© 2020 by Ashley Adana

All rights reserved. No part of this book may be reproduced, distributed, or transmitted in any form or by any means, including photocopying, recording, or other electronic or mechanical methods, without the prior written permission of the publisher, except in the case of brief quotations embodied in critical reviews and certain other noncommercial uses permitted by copyright law. For permission requests, write to Ashley Adana at PO Box 49582, Atlanta, GA 30359.

Disclaimer: Although the author and publisher have made every effort to ensure that the information in this book was correct at press time, the author and publisher do not assume and hereby disclaim any liability to any party for any loss, damage, or disruption caused by errors or omissions, whether such errors or omissions result from negligence, accident, or any other cause. This book is compiled of the author's ideas, concepts, philosophies and opinions. Following the advice in this book could completely transform your life. On the other hand, it may not. So, regardless of the claims throughout this labor of love book – The author and publisher make no claims. Use at your own risk, you accept sole responsibility for the outcomes if you choose to adapt and/or use the content of this book. But honestly, we completely think it will transform your life (in some good ways).

Book Designed by: Rhema Design Co.
Curated & Created by: Ashley Adana
Author Photo: Inije Photography

Printed in the United States of America
First Edition: August 2020
ISBN: 978-1-7354552-3-5
Library of Congress Control Number: 2020913675
AshleyAdana.com
hello@ashleyadana.com

AAM
HOUSE

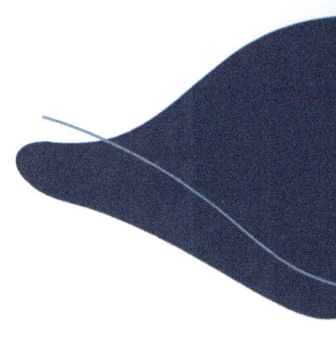

Current Priority:

*365 Empowering Quotes &
Affirmations from Black Voices.
Words to inspire you to choose
yourself daily.*

CURATED & CREATED BY
ASHLEY ADANA

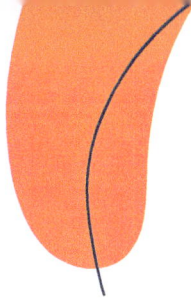

Dedication

Daddy,
Thank you for always telling me I can do anything, and for giving all the advice (solicited and unsolicited) to get it done. I'm so grateful to have embodied the entrepreneurial blood that runs deep in our family tree. I love you, and I will always be your Joy.

Momma,
Girlfriend, you! You've heard me tell you a million times how you show up in my life, but I'll tell you again. My rock, guiding light, shoulder to cry on and stand on, role model, inspiration, sounding board, and best friend. Thank you for your shining presence. I love you.

Pops,
When I open the dictionary and turn to a few words, it's funny that there's a picture of you. Hardworking, provider, heroic, untiring, observant, legendary; yep, your face pops up. Thank you for your unwavering support and love.

Introduction

I'm so grateful you decided to add this little labor of love to your toolbox of inspirational practices. I hope you will use this book to start your day strong and with good intention. The beginning, the start, the takeoff – it's the most important. My mom always tells me, "How you start out is how you hold out." One small positive thing in the morning can change the flow of your whole day. Our thoughts are, indeed, very powerful. Thinking big can make big things happen. But it's not enough to simply think about it. You have to really believe it!

Current Priority: Me is filled with powerful inspirational quotes from black voices including poets, leaders, celebrities, scholars, and my personal tribe. This book is meant to amplify a year of positive thinking, one day at a time. The words will speak to anyone who is pursuing a dream, trying to triumph over adversity, enjoying the beauty that life offers, or on a quest for wholeness. Transforming your mindset with positive thoughts will lead you to positive life changes, which will change the way you show up in the world. Gift yourself energizing words to conquer the day, every day.

I chose to provide you with more than just a quote. Each quote is accompanied by my personal thoughts and ends with an affirmation to help you have victory over the day. This book offers a 365-day journey that will give you strength, wisdom, and an internal fire to move towards the best version of self, each and every day.

Each day, take 15 minutes for yourself, find your favorite quiet place to be alone, grab your cup of coffee (or whatever you like), grab Current Priority: Me, turn to the daily quote, and let it fill your heart and mind. Repeat the daily affirmation for 2 minutes straight and come back to it throughout the day when needed. You got this. It's the beginning (or continuation) of focusing on you!

I hope you enjoy each page and pull strength from the power that lives in our beautiful black voices. Make you a priority, you damn well deserve it!

Love, Ashley Adana
Instagram: @Ashley_Adana

JANUARY 1

If you can't fly then run, if you can't run then walk, if you can't walk then crawl, but whatever you do, you have to keep moving forward.

— Martin Luther King, Jr.

Look for the alternative, look for the modification. No more procrastination, no more excuses. *Stopping isn't the option.*

AFFIRMATION

Today I break old habits that keep me stagnant, and I break new ground with moving forward!

JANUARY 2

I am learning every day to allow the space between where I am and where I want to be to inspire me and not terrify me. It was when I realized I needed to stop trying to be somebody else and be myself, that I actually started to own, accept, and love what I had.

— Tracee Ellis Ross

How powerful is that? Acceptance of self can open up several "self" doors. Self-love, self-awareness, self-care, self-esteem, self-reliance, self-belief, and so many more.

AFFIRMATION

I love and accept myself in this present moment.

JANUARY 3

What counts in life is not the mere fact that we have lived. It is what difference we have made to the lives of others that will determine the significance of the life we lead.

— Nelson Mandela

Your impact doesn't have to meet the masses. Start with being a positive presence for your inner circle. You can inspire them in ways you can't imagine.

AFFIRMATION

I'm grateful for the good I release into my tribe.

JANUARY 4

How many signs it gon' take before it's real for you? Is it too real for you?

— Jidenna

Allow yourself and others to be their authentic selves. If their presence doesn't suit you well, release them. Be ok with them doing the same. We should all be able to show up as our present selves confidently.

AFFIRMATION

I accept myself and others exactly for who they are.

JANUARY 5

Always bet on yourself.

— **Jahi Rawlings**

When you think of a word to describe yourself, use LIMITLESS. Stop trying to force yourself to be small. If you are willing to bet on yourself, you may reap wonderful rewards.

AFFIRMATION

I am focused.

JANUARY 6

We have these rules, the 'hero rules.' Like, a hero doesn't slouch. A hero walks proudly with his head up. A hero walks with a purpose. A hero's always a gentleman.

— John Singleton

Forget the standards of society and others. Our personal standards of greatness are what should guide us. Make yourself proud of yourself.

AFFIRMATION

I have high standards of myself.

JANUARY 7

No place is better than Atlanta. I meant Atlannuh.

— Ashley Adana

I love love love love my city. Yep, I'm a Georgia Peach and wear that badge with honor. I will continue to travel the world, but Atlanta is Home Sweet Home forever. Does your city give you this type of joy too? If so, be a visitor in your own city today. Go support a small business in your neighborhood, take a hike on a new trail or just ride around and enjoy its offerings.

AFFIRMATION

I will enjoy the beauty of my city.

JANUARY 8

A wise man learns from others' mistakes, a fool learns from his own.

— Shannon Sharpe

Life gives us warnings. We have to listen to the whispers before they become screams.

AFFIRMATION

I will listen to signs of the universe with open ears.

JANUARY 9

I have learned not to allow rejection to move me.

— **Cicely Tyson**

Rejection is simply the refusal of a proposal. How many times have you said "no" to something or somebody? Lots, right? Exactly, so you can take a few. Let it roll off like water does on a duck's back.

AFFIRMATION

I won't let rejection shift the crown on my head.

JANUARY 10

Pursue your passions by diving in headfirst.

— **Queen Latifah**

Forget testing the waters, cannon ball into those dreams!

AFFIRMATION

I'm jumping into my future without hesitation.

JANUARY 11

*My responsibility to God is to live.
That's the gift he gave me.*

— **Mary J. Blige**

What a precious gift to receive? Wake up every day with gratitude that you've been given another day.

AFFIRMATION

I'm grateful for the gift of today.

JANUARY 12

Stop trying so hard to be someone you're not.

— **Issa Rae**

Preach, Issa! If we take the necessary time to explore ourselves, we wouldn't have time to research others. Pour your energy into you.

AFFIRMATION

I am dedicated to being the best version of myself.

JANUARY 13

Dreams are lovely. But they are just dreams. fleeting, ephemeral, pretty. But dreams do not come true just because you dream them. It's hard work that makes things happen. It's hard work that creates change.

— Shonda Rhimes

What will you prioritize today for a better tomorrow? Time to take steps to the best chapter of your life.

AFFIRMATION

I will make decisions that will impact the change I desire for my life.

JANUARY 14

It's not about what you tell your children, but how you show them how to live life.

— Jada Pinkett Smith

Their eyes are wide open and focused on you. Children are little sponges taking in the good and the bad.

AFFIRMATION

I embrace the spotlight on me and the eyes watching.

JANUARY 15

Something bigger and better is coming to me. I don't know how and I don't know when, but I know it's coming.

— Aisha Miller

What a word? There is pure excitement in knowing that something great is on the horizon. Those little fuzzies you feel in your stomach that bring a smile to your face, they are real.

AFFIRMATION

My soul is ready to receive my blessing.

JANUARY 16

Failure: Is it a limitation? Bad timing? It's a lot of things. It's something you can't be afraid of, because you'll stop growing. The next step beyond failure could be your biggest success in life.

— Debbie Allen

We all have to experience bumps and bruises of failure, but the possibility of triumph is our desire. We can't pick and choose, we have to embrace it all.

AFFIRMATION

The universe always has my back. I'm going for it.

JANUARY 17

You can't make decisions based on fear and the possibility of what might happen.

— Michelle Obama

Be more afraid of the regret of not trying. Afraid of not asking. Afraid of a mind full of unnecessary wonders.

AFFIRMATION

I will act on the questions in my mind.

JANUARY 18

He who is not courageous enough to take risks will accomplish nothing in life.

— **Muhammad Ali**

If you don't live for experiencing, learning, and truly living... What are you doing?

AFFIRMATION

Today, I will engage in risky behavior to achieve greatness.

JANUARY 19

__Their opinions don't matter. They aren't checks I can deposit into the bank.__

— Ashley Adana

Don't let insignificant people set up shop in your mind. Your brain is like a bank, if people aren't depositing value... it's a no.

AFFIRMATION

They don't matter, I do.

JANUARY 20

We give a lot of others significance in our lives, even when they don't deserve it. It doesn't matter if they're family or if you've known them forever. If they're not good for you, they've got to go.

— **Gabrielle Union**

Release them with ease. Over the years, I've mastered this with pride. I don't allow negativity to swirl around me for long. My peace is top priority in my life, it should be yours too. Don't let anyone disturb that for too long.

AFFIRMATION

I won't allow people who are not good for my soul to occupy space in my life.

JANUARY 21

If you're walking down the right path and you're willing to keep walking, eventually you'll make progress.

— **President Barack Obama**

Keep walking toward the light, it will get brighter and allow you to shine with it.

AFFIRMATION

I'm walking towards greatness.

JANUARY 22

For me, there is a guiding compass that just lives inside of me. Every time I've gone against it, something bad has happened. As long as I stay in line and honor it, it has really been life-changing.

— Tyler Perry

That's your intuition speaking to you, guiding you without hesitation. Honor those feelings and accept their truth.

AFFIRMATION

I trust my journey, and I'm grateful for the helping guides.

JANUARY 23

This morning you woke up. Did you give thanks? Be thankful.

— Iyanla Vanzant

Every day is a chance to be better than yesterday. An opportunity to give a little more to ourselves and others.

AFFIRMATION

I'm grounded in gratitude.

JANUARY 24

Be loyal to those who help you grow. You got a team, you keep your team together, you run as a unit. You got a team of people, it means they believed in you, they bought into your dream. That means they invested into you, they invested time, energy, and effort. In return, you gotta invest your vision, and promise them that we're all going to win together.

— Kevin Hart

Teamwork makes the dream work. This stands true for all relationships in your life: work, family, friends, etc. Support your tribe.

AFFIRMATION

I will support those around me as much as possible.

JANUARY 25

If you don't love it, don't touch it.

— Jenifer Lewis

Such a profound but simple message. I know it's good to try many things to find your thing, but don't stay in something you dislike for long. I look at it as taking up space that doesn't belong to you. You are taking the place of someone who needs to be in that space, and you are not in your love zone. Again, don't stay too long, find your love zone.

AFFIRMATION

I choose to only be in spaces I love.

JANUARY 26

We have to talk about liberating minds as well as liberating society.

— **Angela Davis**

To change our communities, we have to change our mindset. Focus on the things you want to see change with optimism, then create the blueprint to make it reality.

AFFIRMATION

My mind must be free to be focused.

JANUARY 27

> *My thing is that I don't give no person that much power over my path that I'm walking. Not one person can make or break what I'm doing, except me or God.*
>
> — Nipsey Hussle

People will always have opinions on how we walk through OUR lives. You get to choose how much energy you put into their thoughts. Learning to not care will be the most liberating experience you can have. You will move differently when others don't dictate your methods of movement.

AFFIRMATION

I am a master over the path I choose.

JANUARY 28

To be a real man or woman, you've got to know what you believe in. You've got to understand that your actions have consequences and that they are connected to everything that you are.

— **Sister Souljah**

Clarity on how our words and actions affect others is a powerful life tool. We are responsible for how we show up in the world.

AFFIRMATION

My actions matter. I will be conscious of how they affect others.

JANUARY 29

The more you praise and celebrate your life, the more there is in life to celebrate.

— Oprah Winfrey

Celebrate your wins; big or small.

AFFIRMATION

I live my life with gratitude and awareness.

JANUARY 30

I've learned that people will forget what you said, people will forget what you did, but people will never forget how you made them feel.

— Maya Angelou

Marinate on those powerful words.

AFFIRMATION

I will only spread good vibrations to the souls
I touch today.

JANUARY 31

I realized that I don't have to be perfect. All I have to do is show up and enjoy the messy, imperfect, and beautiful journey of my life.

— **Kerry Washington**

Striving for perfection is a losing battle. Accepting that will free you up to live a little more freely.

AFFIRMATION

I'm doing my best and that's enough.

FEBRUARY 1

Thank God for everything! Pray and humbly request your needs to Him; then chill. He's got this! You are well taken care of. Relax, He's in control.

— Orie Lovett Thornton

He will handle it if we release it. We struggle longer when we resist.

AFFIRMATION

I trust with my whole heart that God's in control.

FEBRUARY 2

The reality is: sometimes you lose. And you're never too good to lose. You're never too big to lose. You're never too smart to lose. It happens.

— **Beyoncé**

Find the lesson in each loss. That's where the growth and knowledge lies.

AFFIRMATION

I fully appreciate the lesson in the loss.

FEBRUARY 3

My recipe for life is not being afraid of myself, afraid of what I think or of my opinions.

— Eartha Kitt

We can't be fearful of our own power and weaknesses. They are all significant.

AFFIRMATION

I accept myself for who I am.

FEBRUARY 4

I have learned over the years that when one's mind is made up, this diminishes fear; knowing what must be done does away with fear.

— Rosa Parks

Fear can come from venturing into unknown territory. Scary, right? Well, search for knowledge in that space to make the fear smaller, bit by bit.

AFFIRMATION

My mind is made up. I will seek a deeper knowledge in those things that frighten me.

FEBRUARY 5

A lot of leaders fail because they don't have the bravery to touch that nerve or strike that chord.

— **Kobe Bryant**

Get uncomfortable. Don't ignore that desire to be notable.

AFFIRMATION

I am now bravely living up to my highest potential.

FEBRUARY 6

Words matter, guard your own tongue.

— Donna Pitts

We have to be mindful of the words we speak. Spreading goodness with your words is a gift you can give to the world.

AFFIRMATION

I will be light to the world today, with my words.

FEBRUARY 7

One important key to success is self-confidence. An important key to self-confidence is preparation.

— Arthur Ashe

Showing up as a badass in your designated field means busting your ass in your preparation season.

AFFIRMATION

May I work hard now, to shine bright later.

FEBRUARY 8

Life doesn't stop because something happens to you.

— Magic Johnson

Shit happens and life does too. There will be moments of uncertainty, but they don't last and there's more life to live. Address it and release it.

AFFIRMATION

Today, I will clear my mind and move forward.

FEBRUARY 9

Taking a break, taking a moment, is super important.

— Michael B. Jordan

Sleep in late, keep your PJs on all day, unplug from social media, have a dance party in the living room. You get what I'm saying? Don't do anything that takes energy. Just relax.

AFFIRMATION

Today, I will rest.

FEBRUARY 10

I don't know everything. I know a fraction of what there is to know, and I don't think I will ever know everything, but it's important to me to constantly challenge myself, to understanding different viewpoints, really understanding nuance in topics, so I can feel qualified in what I say, so I'm not preaching falsely of what I'm unaware of.

— Yara Shahidi

In grade school, our teachers told us to study hard for understanding. Well, the same rule applies to adulthood. Lifetime students we are.

AFFIRMATION

I challenge myself to learn more.

FEBRUARY 11

I believe that the love we are born with lurks inside of the most sinister of people.

— Myderia Miller-Tripp

Hate is taught, love is natural. The world needs a consistent flow of love.

AFFIRMATION

I will always choose love.

FEBRUARY 12

Every generation leaves behind a legacy. What that legacy will be is determined by the people of that generation. What legacy do you want to leave behind?

— John Lewis

Choose wisely.

AFFIRMATION

I am a living legacy and I'm mindful of my actions.

FEBRUARY 13

I don't ever remember not having to hustle.

— **Dr. Dre**

Hustle isn't a bad word. It's a daily effort to do more and earn more than you did the day before.

AFFIRMATION

I will work hard today to make my future easier.

FEBRUARY 14

I don't care how high a bird flies, it has to come back down to the ground for water.

— **Alberta Sneid**

This one is from my granny. I listen in awe when she speaks. The Southern wisdom and lessons from her front porch are priceless.

AFFIRMATION

I'm simultaneously humble and confident.

FEBRUARY 15

To reach peace, necessary adjustments have to be made to eliminate stress.

— Ashley Adana

The Lord wants us to find and live in a peaceful space. We are responsible for creating that space.

AFFIRMATION

I have the power to create peace around me.

FEBRUARY 16

Everything you do and every decision you make should be from a place of good. You should always be striving to make the world a better place.

— **Les Brown**

There is evil and good in the world. You get to pick which side you stand on.

AFFIRMATION

I will spread goodness to others.

FEBRUARY 17

I can accept failure. Everyone fails at something. But I can't accept not trying.

— **Michael Jordan**

Don't live with a world of "what ifs." Get on the rollercoaster of life's ups and downs.

AFFIRMATION

I will get on the ride of life. I'm not sitting on the sidelines.

FEBRUARY 18

Hard work and preparation leads to opportunities. Are you ready to take advantage of the opportunity?

— Shantanese Wornum-Miller

Work hard when no one is looking, that's your duty. Others will see the value in your hustle, and the chance to shine on the next level will be granted. Stay the course.

AFFIRMATION

I will enjoy the journey to my next destination.

FEBRUARY 19

Be the King or Queen of your own life, or you will be the pawn in someone else's.

— Aaron Turpeau, Ph.D

Self-love is the leader to all the other "selves" that allow us to move throughout life with confidence. Other selves: self-worth, self-esteem, self-awareness, and self-acceptance.

AFFIRMATION

I acknowledge the self-love I have for myself.

FEBRUARY 20

I always wanted to be someone better the next day than I was the day before.

— Sidney Poitier

Daily progress will get you there.

AFFIRMATION

Every day I am moving towards my better self.

FEBRUARY 21

You've got to learn to leave the table when love's no longer being served.

— Nina Simone

This is just life. Sometimes it calls for us to get up from tables that are comfortable and familiar. If it reeks of negativity and lacks warmth, it's time to exit stage left (or right).

AFFIRMATION

I release everything that is not displaying loving vibes.

FEBRUARY 22

Not everything that is faced can be changed; but nothing can be changed until it is faced.

— James Baldwin

Knowing how to experience change can be a hard one. There is so much comfort in normalcy and routine. But we have to challenge life for change.

AFFIRMATION

I accept the challenge of needed change in my life.

FEBRUARY 23

Wanna fly, you got to give up the shit that weighs you down.

— **Toni Morrison**

Be ok with ending chapters in life. That can be people, places, or things. Release all that does not serve you well. Do it with urgency.

AFFIRMATION

I will digest it, shit it out, flush it away, and keep it moving.

FEBRUARY 24

> *Caring for myself is not self-indulgence, it is self-preservation, and that is an act of political warfare.*
>
> — Audre Lorde

"I'm just so busy" is usually the lie we tell ourselves. Just think about the last time you went to the spa, wasn't that so refreshing? You deserve that feeling often. Do something for you that makes your soul happy.

AFFIRMATION

I am taking time for myself today.

FEBRUARY 25

If there is no struggle, there is no progress.

— Frederick Douglass

My granny says, "You can weather a bad storm, you've seen this before."

AFFIRMATION

I'm embracing my growing pains.

FEBRUARY 26

I'm free. I just do what I want, say what I want, say how I feel, and I don't try to hurt nobody. I just try to make sure that I don't compromise my art in any kind of way, and I think people respect that.

— **Erykah Badu**

The word that Erykah repeats is "I." Your journey is an individual one you share with others who encounter you along the way. Your duty is to enjoy yourself first, then allow others in to get a small taste of the greatness that is you.

AFFIRMATION

I love and accept myself.

FEBRUARY 27

I always believed that when you follow your heart or your gut, when you really follow the things that feel great to you, you can never lose, because settling is the worst feeling in the world.

— Rihanna

Be fearless. Don't hold yourself back.

AFFIRMATION

My dreams deserve a chance.

FEBRUARY 28

God, make me so uncomfortable that I will do the very thing I fear.

— Ruby Dee

Wow! Repeat that 3 times. Bring it on God, I know you have my back.

AFFIRMATION

I trust the Lord.

FEBRUARY 29

I don't do anything until I meditate.

— Russell Simmons

There is power in stillness and meditation. I was introduced to mediation by a dear friend and it's one of the greatest gifts I've ever received. It is a practice. I challenge you to try it for 30 days. Sit down with this book and a journal, give yourself 10 minutes in the morning to get centered, and set your intention for the day. Life changing.

AFFIRMATION

I will be still before I begin my day.

MARCH 1

You may not control all the events that happen to you, but you can decide not to be reduced by them.

— Maya Angelou

Talk about the anxiety and stress that occurs when we try to control the uncontrollable. The tension in your shoulders, your mind, your body; it doesn't deserve it. Release it. Breathe through it.

AFFIRMATION

I am equipped to handle uncomfortable situations.

MARCH 2

You can cage the singer but not the song.

— **Harry Belafonte**

Simply put, Mr. Belafonte.

AFFIRMATION

My voice will be heard, loud and clear.

MARCH 3

You are never too old to reinvent yourself.

— **Steve Harvey**

Never, ever, ever too late. It's never too late to try something that will bring you joy. Erase the negative thought out of your mind.

AFFIRMATION

I have the freedom to change at any time.

MARCH 4

*Don't let what you think you know stop
you from learning what you don't know.*

— Qualena Odom-Royes

Search for full clarity. You don't have all
the answers. There is always room for
improvement and growth.

AFFIRMATION

I will seek better understanding and clarity.

MARCH 5

The only way to get what you really want is to let go of what you don't want.

— Iyanla Vanzant

Sheesh. Simply powerful words.

AFFIRMATION

I will release people, emotions, and things that no longer serve me.

MARCH 6

No matter how bad things are, you can at least be happy that you woke up this morning.

— **D. L. Hughley**

Life can be heavy at times, but we received a gift today; breath in our body to take on the day.

AFFIRMATION

I am grateful for the gift of today.

MARCH 7

Success isn't owned, it's leased. And the rent is due every day.

— LeBron James

Success comes with maintenance requirements. It won't maintain itself.

AFFIRMATION

I strive for victory daily.

MARCH 8

Gospel artists are messengers; they are vessels of a message.

— **Boris Kodjoe**

Boy, can I relate to this being from the South. "The Gospel" as the old folks say, can bring about some needed healing and cleansing. Pick your favorite gospel song and let it resonate through your mind and body. What a feeling! Two of my favorites: Yolanda Adams - "This Battle Is Not Yours" and The New Life Community Choir with John P. Kee - "Thank You Lord (He Did It All)."

AFFIRMATION

I will receive the message through song.

MARCH 9

I'm mad about the waste that happens when people who love each other can't even bring themselves to talk.

— Alice Walker

If your heart was wide open for them before, you can do it again. Lead with love and have the necessary dialogue.

AFFIRMATION

I am going to lead heavy conversations with the initial love felt for them.

MARCH 10

Every great dream begins with a dreamer. Always remember, you have within you the strength, the patience, and the passion to reach for the stars to change the world.

— Harriet Tubman

We have all we need inside of us when we need it most. We have to sometimes dig a little deeper for it, but it's there.

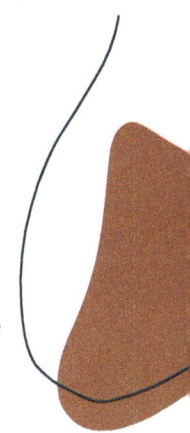

AFFIRMATION

I'm embracing the strength within to soar higher.

MARCH 11

Your playing small does not serve the world. There is nothing enlightened about shrinking so that other people won't feel insecure around you.

— Samuel L. Jackson

Dimming your light, it's not an option.

AFFIRMATION

I will stand proudly in my own light beam.

MARCH 12

You can't stay and go at the same time.

— Ashley Adana

You have to decide which action you will take. Every step in life won't be comfortable, but it will reveal a lesson.

AFFIRMATION

I'm confident in my decision.

MARCH 13

I just want people to feel like they can achieve something great in their lives. We all go through rough times, but love is the antidote. You've got to dream and just believe in yourself. And if you believe, you will achieve it.

— Common

Believe that you can achieve your goals and do good with your time here. Then do the work.

AFFIRMATION

I'm purposeful and impactful.

MARCH 14

Imagine what a harmonious world it could be if every single person, both young and old, shared a little of what he is good at doing.

— Quincy Jones

What a beautiful and wonderous world that would be.

AFFIRMATION

I'm creating a life of passion and purpose to share with the world.

MARCH 15

You are your best thing.

— Toni Morrison

Show up and show out!

AFFIRMATION

I am beautiful. I radiate fierceness.

MARCH 16

I am where I am because of the bridges that I crossed. Sojourner Truth was a bridge. Harriet Tubman was a bridge. Ida B. Wells was a bridge. Madame C. J. Walker was a bridge. Fannie Lou Hamer was a bridge.

— **Oprah Winfrey**

Know the kings and queens that laid the foundation for you. Know your duty is to do it for the next generations.

AFFIRMATION

I am a bridge for the future.

MARCH 17

I was built this way for a reason, so I'm going to use it.

— Simone Biles

Embrace all of your body. See it for the beauty that it is.

AFFIRMATION

I choose to appreciate my body by showering it with love and acceptance.

MARCH 18

Every woman is a queen, and we all have different things to offer.

— Queen Latifah

Show up in all your glory and share it with the world. It needs to know how dope you are.

AFFIRMATION

Today, I will celebrate the Queens in my life, starting with myself.

MARCH 19

My grandmother would say, 'Make sure you look good. Make sure you speak well. Make sure you remain that Southern gentleman that I've taught you to be.'

— Jamie Foxx

We have lessons from wise ones that we carry with us. They are reminders, encouraging us to stay true to who we are.

AFFIRMATION

I will honor the teaching from my ancestors.

MARCH 20

You have to do the research. If you don't know about something, then you ask the right people who do.

— Spike Lee

Six degrees of separation is the idea that everyone is six, or fewer, social connections away from each other. This means your friend knows or has a friend that knows. Just ask, your answer is around the corner.

AFFIRMATION

If I don't know, I will seek the answers.

MARCH 21

I'm rooting for everybody Black!

— Issa Rae

She said what she said. Root for your fellow sisters and brothers to win.

AFFIRMATION

I'm focused on helping others, where and when I can.

MARCH 22

I do what I do. You like it, great. You don't, go listen to somebody else. I'm stickin' with the people who stuck with me.

— Ice Cube

We have to live with acceptance of self, and love on those who love on us.

AFFIRMATION

I'm surrounded with positive people who love me and are willing to help bring out the best in me.

MARCH 23

God will and has always made a way.

— Ashley Adana

He is the ultimate source.

AFFIRMATION

I'm always on God's mind.

MARCH 24

You can never be upset with the people who forced you into your dream.

— **Tyler Perry**

Thank the ones who said you couldn't. They just added fuel to your burning flame.

AFFIRMATION

To my haters, your doubt fuels me. Thank You.

MARCH 25

I have discovered in life that there are ways of getting almost anywhere you want to go, if you really want to go.

— Langston Hughes

Light a fire under your butt! If you want to meet that goal, you have to write the blueprint to get there. It's go time.

AFFIRMATION

From this moment forward, I invite unlimited abundance into my life.

MARCH 26

If somebody's going to invest hundreds of thousands of dollars, even more into you, you want to make sure you can return that; you want to make sure they feel good about their investment.

— Ari Lennox

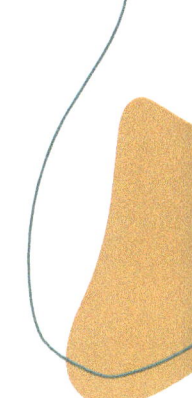

Our ancestors sacrificed their lives, money, time, and more for a better tomorrow for us. Let their ROI be bountiful.

AFFIRMATION

I'm the governor over my inheritance, and I will use it responsibly.

MARCH 27

Compromising for what? Compromising for what reason? What is compromise?

— **Eartha Kitt**

This makes my heart smile. The definition of compromise is to accept standards that are lower than desirable. Why do we compromise and settle in so many areas of our lives?

AFFIRMATION

I value being honest to myself, and I will not compromise on my beliefs.

MARCH 28

Hard to move on when you always regret one.

— **J. Cole**

Moving on can be hard, right? Accepting the reality of the thing you regret is key. The healing is in the release.

AFFIRMATION

I forgive myself for holding onto regret for too long.

MARCH 29

Have a vision. Be demanding.

— **Colin Powell**

The universe is working in your favor, trust that. You just keep working the plan.

AFFIRMATION

I believe the universe is on my side.

MARCH 30

You have to experience life, make observations, and ask questions.

— **Yasiin Bey**

Ask questions relentlessly and search for adventure constantly.

AFFIRMATION

I commit to an inquisitive life.

MARCH 31

Self-love has very little to do with how you feel about your outer self. It's about accepting all of yourself.

— Tyra Banks

Positive self-talk is the only chatter you should be speaking to yourself. You should praise the goodness of all aspects that are you.

AFFIRMATION

I love the masterpiece I am.

APRIL 1

Love and build, love and work, love and fight. Always love first. Anything placed before love will fail.

— **Sister Souljah**

So true. Lead with love and it will flow back to you without a doubt.

AFFIRMATION

I will begin all things with love.

APRIL 2

God is ever present. He's in every breath, in every step. He's here, always, always.

— Jill Scott

Sometimes God is the ONLY support you have. Guess what? He is sufficient. Lean on him. Nurture that relationship. He is our Almighty God and Provider.

AFFIRMATION

I will rest in the presence of God.

APRIL 3

I've always had confidence. It came because I have lots of initiative. I wanted to make something of myself.

— Eddie Murphy

You are the only person who can light and feel the fire within your soul. You are the designer of your desired life. Get back to work and create the life you want.

AFFIRMATION

I will carve out the tailored life of my dreams.

APRIL 4

My mission in life is not merely to survive, but to thrive; and to do so with some passion, some compassion, some humor, and some style.

— Maya Angelou

As children, we worked hard and strived to get a gold star from our teacher. Same applies to adulthood; continue the yearn for that feeling. We have more to do than just exist.

AFFIRMATION

Today, I will focus on what I want to attract into my life.

APRIL 5

I'm just very thankful. And I say that a lot because that's the most important message.

— Pharrell Williams

Take a few minutes to speak 5 things you are thankful for. Sit with those things. I'm sure you're smiling from the joy they bring you.

AFFIRMATION

I am thankful for my life.

APRIL 6

All business is personal… Make your friends before you need them.

— Robert L. Johnson

People do business with people. Support those around you when you can. It's not always about spending your dollars. It can be your time, your presence, or your prayers.

AFFIRMATION

I will do my best to support those I care for.

APRIL 7

It doesn't matter if a million people tell you what you can't do, or if ten million people tell you no. If you get one yes from God, that's all you need.

— Tyler Perry

God is the only validator I seek. If anyone believes in me, that's a bonus. Look around, the evidence is there: People pleasing is a pain prison.

AFFIRMATION

God's approval is all I need.

APRIL 8

As I rise every morning, I thank the Lord for keeping us safe; me, my family and my friends. I praise his Holy Name because he is worthy of praise.

— Francis Pruitt

Did you catch that last part? He is worthy of your praise.

AFFIRMATION

I thank God for his grace and mercy over my life.

APRIL 9

When I find myself having that much trouble with a song or a character or a story, I tend to move on.

— Jazmine Sullivan

Let's apply this to scenarios in everyday life. An excessive and constant disturbance of peace is a great reason for dismissal. I'm not saying you won't have hardships, but misery should not have a place in your presence.

AFFIRMATION

I deny any need for suffering and misery. I deserve the best.

APRIL 10

I'm at peace with what I'm doing, I feel good with what I wake up doing and about my lifestyle.

— Nipsey Hussle

This is such a powerful place to be in! We should all strive for this peacefulness.

AFFIRMATION

I am content with my life, my heart, and my mind.

APRIL 11

I stay in tune with my family and God.

— **Regina King**

Family can sometimes be your best accountability partner. They give you the room to be free, hold you accountable for your mess, and love on you at the same time.

AFFIRMATION

I will continue to be humble and my authentic self.

APRIL 12

Character is power.

— Booker T. Washington

Your thoughts, beliefs, motives, and behaviors all go into the pot of a stew called you. Be sure it's a recipe of goodness.

AFFIRMATION

I am responsible for my own attitude.

APRIL 13

*I've always tried to work hard
and stay focused, and just use one
opportunity to contribute to the next.*

— T.I. Harris

Your next golden opportunity is around the corner. Keep working with the highest level of integrity. It's coming.

AFFIRMATION

I have faith that good things are on the horizon for me.

APRIL 14

True love accepts you where you are, helps you get where you need to be, and will not tear you down when you get where you were predestined to be.

— Andrea Smith

This is the type of love you should expect from yourself and require from others. Give the gift of self love, then share it with others.

AFFIRMATION

I am worthy to receive true love in all stages of my growth.

APRIL 15

The future rewards those who press on. I don't have time to feel sorry for myself. I don't have time to complain. I'm going to press on.

— President Barack Obama

Your reminder today is to keep moving forward. Your desires are on the horizon.

AFFIRMATION

I won't let anything stand in the way of tomorrow's success.

APRIL 16

It's gotta work or it's gotta work.

— Nehemiah Davis

There are no other options available. Your plan is going to work because you are working it. Don't change your goal, change your blueprint to reach it.

AFFIRMATION

I am going to win by any means necessary.

APRIL 17

Let no man pull you so low as to hate him.

— **Martin L. King Jr.**

You know you're in control of your emotions, right? Step away, breathe, and process those feelings. Stay aligned with the goodness in you.

AFFIRMATION

Today, I will take the high road.

APRIL 18

You're flawless when you embrace the things about you that you don't necessarily like, but you own them because they're yours.

— Amanda Seales

Enough said.

AFFIRMATION

I lovingly accept myself exactly as I am.

APRIL 19

Unfuckwithable is the mood for the day.

— Ashley Adana

Put on your crown and conquer the day.

AFFIRMATION

Today, I choose...ME.

APRIL 20

What doesn't kill you will make you stronger.

— **Leigh Meriweather Knight**

Some negative things will happen in your life. It will feel like a ton of bricks on your heart and shoulders. But know this, your breakdown will be followed by a breakthrough. Believe it.

AFFIRMATION

I find strength in the lessons of life.

APRIL 21

A snail's pace is still moving. Keep going!

— Ashley Adana

Don't hesitate, keep moving and you will get there in due time.

AFFIRMATION

I won't give up. Every step forward counts.

APRIL 22

Don't let anyone convince you that your dream, your vision to be an entrepreneur, is something that you shouldn't do. What often happens is that people who are well meaning, who really care for us, are afraid for us and talk us out of it.

— Cathy Hughes

This applies to any career, hobby, or interest you have. Please try it, just try. Don't listen to anyone who tells you that it's impossible. Take it one step further and stop talking to those people who pull you away from things or ideas that make your heart sing.

AFFIRMATION

I won't let anyone stand in the way of my future success or happiness.

APRIL 23

*The only time you should look back in life,
is to see how far you have come.*

— **Kevin Hart**

Have you ever heard of scoreboard watching? It's when you constantly keep an eye on the past wins in life. It's a distraction, stop it. Celebrate the win in the moment then move on to the next goal.

AFFIRMATION

Thank you yesterday for your joy, it's time to focus on today.

APRIL 24

Trust the wait and enjoy your becoming journey.

— Ashley Adana

As we live in a microwave world where most things are fast, we have to find the enjoyment of being patient in some areas of life. Depend on God for guidance and strength during the journey.

AFFIRMATION

I will be patient with myself to enjoy all of today's moments.

APRIL 25

Just don't give up what you're trying to do. Where there is love and inspiration, I don't think you can go wrong.

— Ella Fitzgerald

Giving up on what your heart tells you isn't an option.

AFFIRMATION

Today, what serves me gets to stay, and what doesn't has to go!

APRIL 26

I will not lose, for even in defeat, there's a valuable lesson learned, so it evens up for me.

— Jay-Z

I love the perspective Jay-Z shares on losing. Find the lesson in the lost, that's the gem.

AFFIRMATION

My struggles are opportunities to grow and learn.

APRIL 27

Hate is too great a burden to bear. It injures the hater more than it injures the hated.

— **Coretta Scott King**

Hate on another for what? No time for that bad karma. I'm too busy anyway lol! Hate isn't in my heart.

AFFIRMATION

I only have love to give.

APRIL 28

I don't play tag, bitch. I been it.

— Lizzo

Be bold in how you show up in the world. We need all of you. Stay true to you at all times.

AFFIRMATION

My only competition is myself.

APRIL 29

Thinking is action, but there is nothing on this Earth as powerful as consistent, bold, physical action. When you take action, particularly bold action, the boundaries of what you believe to be possible expand.

— Victor Durrah Jr.

Rock the boat, take the risk! No playing it small today. Boldness is the only option.

AFFIRMATION

I am bold. I have the courage to take risks that shape my future for the better.

APRIL 30

A problem is a chance for you to do your best.

— Duke Ellington

Your best is all you can give and that's sufficient.

AFFIRMATION

I'm going to do my best to solve problems with integrity and grace.

MAY 1

If you're afraid to fail, then you're probably going to fail.

— **Kobe Bryant**

Have you ever been so scared of failure that you decided not to try it at all? Don't self-sabotage your upcoming wins.

AFFIRMATION

I have conquered too much to compromise now.

MAY 2

Like most people, I've had several awakenings.

— **Jidenna**

There is no way you can plan for an awakening. They stubble into your life and shake everything up. It's that feeling when you are sitting with a perplexed frown on your face, that turns into a raised eyebrow, that leads to a smile and head nod. It's that "now I get it" feeling. It seems that awakenings occur at the right time, when you need them most.

AFFIRMATION

I will cherish my "aha" moments.

MAY 3

I walk in the strength of the Lord.

— Jason Taylor

What a mighty friend we have in God. When your relationship is active and aligned, you are given the power you need to journey life with purpose and fulfillment.

AFFIRMATION

I have victory over all. The Lord is with me at all times.

MAY 4

With growth comes wisdom and success. Never allow life to become stagnant.

— **Derrick Miller, Sr.**

Standing still isn't an option. Push yourself, push your mind, push your own boundaries.

AFFIRMATION

I strive to grow every day.

MAY 5

Dissociation is stronger than revenge.

— **Anika Miller**

No need to battle with people, places, or things that no longer serve you. Not giving a damn is better than revenge too.

AFFIRMATION

I'm done, done, done.

MAY 6

I try my best to confront situations because I know, at the end of the day, you can deal with it or it will deal with you. I've had enough experience to know that that's how it goes down. There's no going around it.

— Jada Pinkett Smith

Address it today, it has no place for tomorrow, and you damn sure can't take it into next year. Go ahead, tackle the beast.

AFFIRMATION

I will deal with the unsettling matters in my life for resolution.

MAY 7

*But I always had the ability to say no.
That's how I called my own shots.*

— Sidney Poitier

It's time to go waaaaaay back to your terrible twos and use that famous word, NO. Toddlers use "no" with confidence and conviction, right? OK adults, let's say it together, NO! There is power in yes, but there's also power in no.

AFFIRMATION

I have the power to say no.

MAY 8

If you have children who love and respect you, this too can be a sign of your success.

— Les Brown

You don't have to put on a cape to have superpowers in their eyes. Your presence, personal happiness, love, and consistency is all the power you need.

AFFIRMATION

Being a parent gives me great joy, and I'm doing my best.

MAY 9

Don't throw rail for rail.

— Alberta Sneid

Another Granny-ism for you. This means the same as the famous Michelle Obama quote, "When they go low, we go high." Don't allow someone else's actions to get you out of character.

AFFIRMATION

I am accountable for my words and actions.

MAY 10

> *I think a role model is a mentor – someone you see on a daily basis, and you learn from them.*
>
> — Denzel Washington

My mother, momma, mom, mommy, MVP, BFF, Black Beauty Queen, Mrs. Miller-Tripp. Yep, that's my role model. She has taught me priceless lessons, shown me overflowing love, and gave me needed ass whoopins lol. For all of that, I'm blessed beyond measure. Give your mentor a call today, send a bouquet of flowers, or take them out for lunch.

AFFIRMATION

Today, I will show my mentors I love them.

MAY 11

All of us should be much more humble and contrite when we point the finger at somebody else, because four more fingers are pointing back at us.

— Michael Eric Dyson

Release your judgement towards yourself and others. When you judge someone, you may be missing the opportunity to get to know who they are and how you can help.

AFFIRMATION

I choose not to criticize myself or others.

MAY 12

What would you do if you weren't afraid?

— **Steve Harvey**

Well damn. Good question, Steve. I had to sit with this one for a few minutes. I want you to do the same.

AFFIRMATION

I release any fear limiting me. It has no place in my life.

MAY 13

I'm always moving forward.

— **Debbie Allen**

All day, every day.

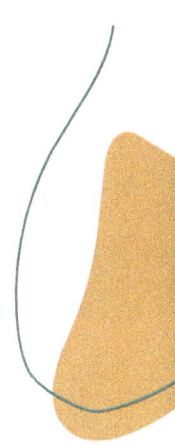

AFFIRMATION

My life is in progressive mode and full of amazing opportunities.

MAY 14

Lord, please open my heart to accept things in plain sight, good and bad. Allow me to see and receive them clearly to make mindful decisions.

— Ashley Adana

This is a prayer I say to myself when my heart and mind are pulling in different directions. Feel free to use it.

AFFIRMATION

I accept what is, with no resistance.

MAY 15

You can't just sit there and wait for people to give you that golden dream. You've got to get out there and make it happen for yourself.

— Diana Ross

Don't sit around looking for hookups and handouts. Dreams don't work unless you do.

AFFIRMATION

What I want is within my reach and I'm totally committed.

MAY 16

You don't have to hold onto the pain to hold onto the memory.

— Janet Jackson

It's ok to allow the negative emotions to flow through you. However, you have to allow them to move through, don't allow them to live there.

AFFIRMATION

I'm allowed to feel all of my emotions.

MAY 17

To be yourself is truly a revolutionary act, and I think more and more people should try it, because it's gotten me a pretty cool life.

— Lena Waithe

No apologies necessary. Share yourself boldly and with pride.

AFFIRMATION

I'm unashamedly me.

MAY 18

> *When you don't show up as who you are, people fall in love with who you're not. Then when they find out who you are, that's when they leave.*
>
> — Iyanla Vanzant

There is not one person out there like you. You are uniquely designed, and that's what you need to share with the world. Your tribe will gravitate toward you, and you will feel the unwavering love they have to offer.

AFFIRMATION

I accept myself for who I truly am.

MAY 19

Education is the passport to the future, for tomorrow belongs to those who prepare for it today.

— Malcolm X

Education is an important survival tool that is accessible to all. The world wide web is a free-flowing collection of knowledge. We don't have a reason to ever stop seeking new knowledge.

AFFIRMATION

I am excited to learn something new today.

MAY 20

Never be afraid to sit awhile and think.

— **Lorraine Hansberry**

My mom always tells me to stop and think before responding. With age and experience, I'm getting better at this every day. When we give ourselves the time we need to process our feelings, we can deliver the message better.

AFFIRMATION

I am not in a rush. I accept that sometimes things just take longer than planned.

MAY 21

Keep trying. Persistence and consistency is the best thing. As long as you keeping it real, and you keep trying, keep banging that wall and it will fall.

— **Christopher "Biggie Smalls" Wallace**

You've got this! Stay on purpose. Stay on task.

AFFIRMATION

Quitting isn't an option. I'm committed to the pursuit.

MAY 22

I've always been one to take chances, and I've always been one to, to create or follow through with instincts.

— Teddy Pendergrass

Your inner voice is valid. Listen up.

AFFIRMATION

I will follow my heart and instincts.

MAY 23

What I have learned in this life is, you can never be ashamed of where you come from.

— **Tyler Perry**

Denying your past will not allow you to live freely in your present. Even if the past brings you more darkness than light, acknowledge it. Your past has brought you to this very moment, your beautiful present.

AFFIRMATION

I acknowledge my ups and downs, as they have made me who I am.

MAY 24

I don't feel as though I have to prove anything to anybody.

— **Patti LaBelle**

I know that's right, Patti! You agree, right?

AFFIRMATION

The only validator in my life is me.

MAY 25

Don't be afraid of elevation, take chances. In other words, don't be afraid of heights.

— Monde Williams

Go above and beyond your comfort level. On your job, in your business, with your hobbies. Going the extra mile in all you do allows you to reach new heights naturally.

AFFIRMATION

I'm not afraid to raise the bar and set new standards for myself.

MAY 26

Everything we do should be a result of our gratitude for what God has done for us.

— Lauryn Hill

God will make a way; he is our guide. Every day, give gratitude.

AFFIRMATION

I am in harmony with all that God provides for me. I am thankful.

MAY 27

When the OutKast sound changed and I started producing my own records, I would mirror what I thought that character doing that music would look like. As the sound got a little wilder, freakier and funkier, so did the clothes. Then when the sound got more sophisticated, the clothes changed again.

— Andre "3000" Benjamin

Embrace the different chapters you will experience on this journey called life. Each chapter will have different versions of you, as it should.

AFFIRMATION

I will accept the evolution of self.

MAY 28

It is a full-time job being honest one moment at a time, remembering to love, to honor, to respect. It is a practice, a discipline, worthy of every moment.

— Jasmine Guy

Practice makes perfect, that's the cliché.
Practice makes you an expert, that's the truth.

AFFIRMATION

I choose to practice honesty daily.

MAY 29

*When you put love out in the world,
it travels, and it can touch people and
reach people in ways that we never
even expected.*

— Laverne Cox

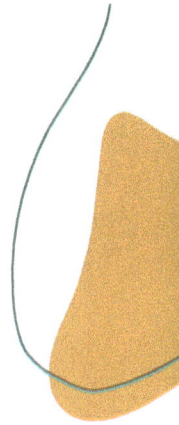

Everything you do is a choice. You are in
control of the spirit you give to the world.
Give goodness.

AFFIRMATION

I commit to spreading love.

MAY 30

I want a world where everything is welcome, everything is valid, everything is acknowledged, embraced, and accepted. To me, that's a perfect world.

— CeeLo Green

Everyone has the right to show up in life the way they choose to. That's the beauty of society; we are all uniquely contributing the best way we know how.

AFFIRMATION

I will embrace and accept others' differences.

Hold on to your dreams of a better life and stay committed to striving to realize it.

— **Earl G. Graves, Sr.**

Your current thinking and actions are molding your future. Keep striving for the best, you deserve it.

AFFIRMATION

I see the beauty in my future.

JUNE 1

None of us alone can save the nation or the world. But each of us can make a positive difference if we commit ourselves to do so.

— **Cornel West**

We're all in this together. We all have obligations to be impactful. It doesn't have to be to the masses, it can be in your own family or your job.

AFFIRMATION

I commit to displaying the positivity I want to see in the world.

JUNE 2

Lessons learned in life are everywhere if you choose to open the book.

— Gail Johnson

The universe communicates with you. You decide if you are willing to listen and understand its messages.

AFFIRMATION

I choose to listen as life speaks to me.

JUNE 3

When people feel some kind of way about you doing what's right, it's their problem, not yours.

— Myderia Miller-Tripp

People pleasing is not on the agenda. If you feel good about how you show up in the world, that's a good reason to sleep well at night. Keep doing you!

AFFIRMATION

I'm in the right place, doing the right thing, at the right time.

JUNE 4

I believe in prayer. It's the best way we have to draw strength from heaven.

— **Josephine Baker**

The power of prayer, sheeesh. Spiritual power, what a beautiful gift to receive. When you spend time connecting to the Almighty, your spiritual strength will be activated.

AFFIRMATION

I am aware of my strength coming from above and within.

JUNE 5

You must be bold, brave, and courageous and find a way... to get in the way.

— John Lewis

Sometimes you have to shake things up and have a bold presence to see the change you desire. Sometimes you have to step on those toes, then look back and say, "Excuse me."

AFFIRMATION

I will boldly take action to achieve my goals.

JUNE 6

You're not obligated to win. You're obligated to keep trying to do the best you can every day.

— Marian Wright Edelman

It's possible to do enough to get by, but the challenge is in doing your best. Do you accept the challenge?

AFFIRMATION

Today is an opportunity to do my best.

JUNE 7

Everything will change. The only question is growing up or decaying.

— Nikki Giovanni

Change is inevitable, growth is a choice.
Fertilize what and where you want to grow.

AFFIRMATION

I will not wilt away, but grow upward.

JUNE 8

There's a thing you confront when you're going into something new and you come to this sort of abyss, and then you push yourself. It makes you try different things.

— **Forest Whitaker**

Take a deep breath, release the resistance you feel, and embrace the newness.

AFFIRMATION

Today, I'm going to push myself outside of my comfort zone.

JUNE 9

You don't have to be one of those people that accepts things as they are. Every day, take responsibility for changing them right where you are.

— **Cory Booker**

"Oh well, that's just life." Nooooo, no. You aren't stuck. First, change your outlook, then change your actions.

AFFIRMATION

I am totally in charge of the change I want for my life.

JUNE 10

When you are kind to someone in trouble, you hope they'll remember and be kind to someone else. And it'll become like a wildfire.

— **Whoopi Goldberg**

Kindness, compassion, and empathy for others is the foundation to spreading love. We can change the world when we lead with them.

AFFIRMATION

I touch others with a kindhearted approach.

JUNE 11

Surrender without questions.

— Ashley Adana

This is a hard one for me because I'm a planner and calculated thinker. I think about start to finish and everything in between, which has stopped me from pursuing things that are in my heart. I'm still a work in progress on this one.

AFFIRMATION

I will let my heart lead the way.

JUNE 12

*No temporary chaos is worth
your sanity.*

— **Nasir Jones**

Don't make permanent decisions based on temporary emotions. This doesn't mean your emotions aren't valid, but your peace doesn't have to be sacrificed. Take a step back, breathe, and then proceed.

AFFIRMATION

I know this too shall pass.

JUNE 13

Stop running to those who ignore you and start running to those who adore you.

— Russell Simmons

I say this very casually, but I know it's hard for some to do.... cut them loose. If you aren't receiving compassion and genuine concern from someone, they shouldn't be a recipient of your time, energy, or presence.

AFFIRMATION

I deserve to be surrounded by those who care for me deeply.

JUNE 14

One of the most beautiful things in the world I've ever seen or heard is people laughing, even when there seems to be so little reason for them to laugh.

— D. L. Hughley

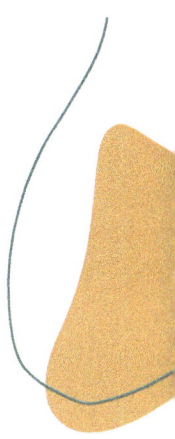

Laughter is good medicine. Take your daily dose.

AFFIRMATION

I am a magnet for joy and laughter.

JUNE 15

I think the worst thing you can do about a situation is nothing.

— Ice Cube

Have you heard of a good, clean fight? Yes, we all experience discomfort in life, but we have to use effective tools to manage the atmosphere. "Fighting clean" means having purposeful dialogue to preserve (not damage) the relationship while expressing disagreement with another person. Take some time to research clean fighting and give it a try. This has been a game changer for how I resolve conflict in life.

AFFIRMATION

I will enter difficult conversations with an open mind and heart.

JUNE 16

Death is not the greatest loss in life. The greatest loss is what dies inside while still alive. Never surrender.

— Tupac Shakur

Protect that flame burning inside of you. Some days may be harder than others, but let that fire shine.

AFFIRMATION

I am unstoppable. I am determined to make my goals my reality.

JUNE 17

Forgiving is easy. Trusting again, not so much.

— Kendrick Lamar

You've conquered and survived 100% of everything in your life thus far, so there's a pretty good chance you'll survive whatever else is placed in your life. Resentment has no place in your heart. Forgive, heal the hurt, then trust the next freely.

AFFIRMATION

I allow the energy of forgiveness to surround me.

JUNE 18

You can't tell me what I can't do anymore.

— **Ava DuVernay**

Knowing your responsibility and rights to the space you take up is supreme. You are the writer of your life, no one else.

AFFIRMATION

I honor my purpose.

JUNE 19

Everything you do, every thought you have, every word you say, creates a memory that you will hold in your body. It's imprinted on you and affects you in subtle ways - ways you are not always aware of. With that in mind, be very conscious and selective.

— Phylicia Rashad

Feeding goddess into our thoughts is essential for all areas of our lives.

AFFIRMATION

I will be conscious of my thoughts about myself and others.

JUNE 20

There's no such thing as can't! Anything you want in life is on the other side of discipline and consistency.

— **Janel Grant-Hanserd**

Remove that negative thought bubble from your mind. Being aware of your thoughts is the first step to moving towards what's meant for you.

AFFIRMATION

I am not limiting myself with negative talk.

JUNE 21

Replace the.... fear, lack of knowledge, and anxiety with ... excitement, eagerness, and gratitude for the next chapter.

— Ashley Adana

We have to be willing to live in the unlimited goodness of the future, not the fear of it.

AFFIRMATION

I willingly accept my past, and eagerly anticipate my bright future.

JUNE 22

I used to want the words 'She tried' on my tombstone. Now I want 'She did it.'

— **Katherine Dunham**

What's your shining goal? The goal that will allow you to shine bright for all to notice. Don't play small, get on the path to achieve it.

AFFIRMATION

I will live an abundant and prosperous life.

JUNE 23

__Winning is great, sure, but if you are really going to do something in life, the secret is learning how to lose. Nobody goes undefeated all the time. If you can pick up after a crushing defeat, and go on to win again, you are going to be a champion someday.__

— Wilma Rudolph

Mindset is a major key to succeeding. Knowing you gain and lose are life lessons we've all experienced. Remember as a child, when you didn't make the cut for the team or the puppy love breakup? Adulthood isn't any different. We have to take the wins and failures dealt.

AFFIRMATION

I have the mind of a champion. I can endure it all.

JUNE 24

When you take care of yourself, you're a better person for others. When you feel good about yourself, you treat others better.

— Solange Knowles

Wake up every morning loving on yourself, praising yourself, then go share that love with the world.

AFFIRMATION

My day begins and ends with self-love.

JUNE 25

I live in the space of thankfulness — and for that, I have been awarded a million times over. I started out giving thanks for small things, and the more thankful I became, the more my bounty increased. That's because — for sure — what you focus on expands. When you focus on the goodness in life, you create more of it.

— **Oprah Winfrey**

When we aren't good stewards and thankful for the small treasures in life, how could we treasure the bounty? To have a life of abundance, you have to start with filling your heart with gratitude for modest moments.

AFFIRMATION

My life is a gift, and I appreciate everything I've received.

JUNE 26

People don't need you, but they'll sure as hell use ya.

— **Shannon Sharpe**

Any relationship (biz or personal) will be give and take. Be sure you feel good about what you are giving and what you are receiving back.

AFFIRMATION

I will examine my relationships to be sure they work well for me.

JUNE 27

Change doesn't have to be hard, and healing doesn't have to hurt. Surely by now you know that everything happens for a reason. There is something better awaiting you on the other side of this.

— Iyanla Vanzant

So true. We have some practice in the department of heartaches. We are equipped to process it and move forward. So, that's what we will do.

AFFIRMATION

I know there is purpose in the lesson, and I understand it.

JUNE 28

Rejection is usually God's protection.

— Hill Harper

Acknowledge how you feel. Rejection is a hard one because it's usually tied to a desire of something you wanted in your life. It is important that you allow yourself some time to grieve the lost but also sit in the reality that it wasn't meant for you.

AFFIRMATION

Thank you for releasing things that ain't meant for me.

JUNE 29

> *It's not the load that breaks you down, it's the way you carry it.*
>
> — Lena Horne

Plant your feet firmly on the ground, get your footing then proceed forward. You got this!

AFFIRMATION

I'm ready and equipped to carry the load of today.

JUNE 30

If you stay small enough, long enough, God will make you big enough, soon enough.

— **Dr. E. Dewey Smith, Jr.**

I love this one from Dr. Smith. This is a mighty word he often shares with the church. Do work from your heart, with passion and purpose. If you stay obedient to the task of sowing the seed, the harvest will be bountiful.

AFFIRMATION

I am focused on my duty of sowing.

JULY 1

Don't let anyone steal ya joy! There's always someone miserable trying to bring you down ... you just wish them well and proceed on enjoying your life.

— Missy Elliott

You know the saying, hurt people hurt people. We will all encounter pain from others, but we get to determine how long they get to cause it. You know your tolerance level, honor it.

AFFIRMATION

I forgive all who have inflicted pain onto me.

JULY 2

For people to be able to sit down together and have a conversation, that's the power of love.

— Jada Pinkett Smith

Converse for understanding. The goal is to listen with an open heart and ears. Turn toward the person who is talking, lean in, look them in the eyes and listen.

AFFIRMATION

I'm willing to be a good listener for someone in need.

JULY 3

There is no greater agony than bearing an untold story inside you.

— Maya Angelou

Honor your voice. Speak outwards. You are giving a gift to yourself and possibly others without even knowing it. There is true value in your words.

AFFIRMATION

My voice is worthy of being shared and heard.

JULY 4

Everyone is figuring out this thing called life.

— **Ashley Adana**

We need to allow ourselves to make mistakes, have uncomfortable conversations, and embrace pain. It helps us shift things/attitudes/actions for the positive.

AFFIRMATION

I will be kind to myself and have compassion for others.

JULY 5

Your name is the most important thing you possess. Treat and protect it as a rare gem. It will never lose its value.

— Stephanie Daniels

Your birthright is to honor and appreciate yourself. Do so on a daily basis.

AFFIRMATION

I respect and honor the legacy I am creating.

JULY 6

Laughter heals all wounds, and that's one thing that everybody shares. No matter what you're going through, it makes you forget about your problems. I think the world should keep laughing.

— **Kevin Hart**

Yield to the pain, then put on your favorite comedy movie. That's one dose of healing.

AFFIRMATION

I will let laughter lead the way.

JULY 7

When you really believe in God, it gives you a courage, a confidence that enables you to meet the things coming.

— **Della Reese**

Faith is confidence is God. If you have it, you are armored up! In weak moments, go back to that word, FAITH!

AFFIRMATION

God has equipped me for things I will encounter.

JULY 8

I don't think you can measure wealth in dollars and cents. I really don't believe that at all because there are some things that money cannot buy. One of them is health. And the other is security in your relationships and friends.

— **Cicely Tyson**

The great riches in life aren't monetary. They're our family, friends, careers and passion projects. Let gratitude lay in those things.

AFFIRMATION

I'm grateful for the treasures in my life, my health and my loved ones.

JULY 9

I'd rather be happy being myself than sad trying to please everyone else.

— J. Cole

If you like the reflection in the mirror, you're good. Don't let others' thoughts hold you back from living your good life.

AFFIRMATION

I accept all of myself.

JULY 10

*The progress of the world will call for
the best that all of us have to give.*

— Mary McLeod Bethune

GIVING YOUR BEST and GIVING are different.
100% and 90% are different. When you give
100%, that's the Full Monty.

AFFIRMATION

I'm giving the world my BEST today.

JULY 11

Welcome the constant shifting of what is life.

— Ashley Adana

Becoming is a lifetime process, enjoy the ride. It has been said, "Life is like the ocean. It can be calm and still or rough and rigid, but in the end, it is always beautiful."

AFFIRMATION

I welcome the waves in my life.

JULY 12

May we help more than we hurt, may we seek to understand more than be understood and may we love more than we judge.

— **Cory Booker**

Such a great reminder of how to live with a servant heart. Inspiring others to have healthy mental and emotional strength is a real gift.

AFFIRMATION

Today, I will give encouraging words to others.

JULY 13

*Success is liking yourself, liking what
you do, and liking how you do it.*

— Maya Angelou

Now that's euphoria. I want this for all of us,
so keep falling in love with yourself. It's totally
achievable. Go for it.

AFFIRMATION

I'm proud of myself. I'm happy and free being me.

JULY 14

Life is real, it's not going to be smooth.

— **Mary J. Blige**

We all have to learn and grow through all phases of life. Those hard times may be really bumpy, but you will reign as you always have.

AFFIRMATION

I have unwavering faith that everything will be fine.

JULY 15

> *I keep my back against the wall so I can see my friends and foes coming towards me.*

— Vincent Hall

The ability to see the full landscape is an advantage. It provides you the opportunities to see clearly and make the right decision for you.

AFFIRMATION

I see right through illusions; my vision is clear.

JULY 16

Do you know how powerful you are?

— **Sean "Diddy" Combs**

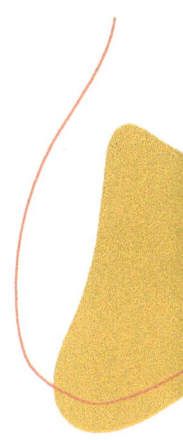

The power is you! Break through the limitations you put on yourself.

AFFIRMATION

I am a force and I live fearlessly.

JULY 17

*If you're not invited to the party,
throw your own.*

— **Diahann Carroll**

Party of one! Being with yourself and celebrating yourself is mandatory. You can't care for others and neglect yourself. Move your name to the top of the list.

AFFIRMATION

I see the beauty in being with myself.

JULY 18

No one is born hating another person because of the color of his skin, or his background, or his religion. People must learn to hate, and if they can learn to hate, they can be taught to love, for love comes more naturally to the human heart than its opposite.

— Nelson Mandela

If you have inherited actions/traits that harm and hurt others, release them. Each and every one of us deserves to have intense love throughout our lifetime.

AFFIRMATION

Others are worthy of my heart and empathy. I'm worthy of their love and embrace.

JULY 19

If you go through life, and you don't find the beauty in an unexpected place, then you really have a sad existence.

— Octavia Spencer

If it's time to undergo emotional surgery, today is the day. No more existing, it's time for you to live. Life has so much to offer us that can bring us joy. Write down 3 things that bring a smile to your face. Go do one of them, no hesitation and no excuses. Then tomorrow, the day after, and forever, do the same.

AFFIRMATION

Today, I gift myself a little piece of joy.

JULY 20

I'm not good at everything, I just do my best at everything.

— Michael B. Jordan

You have to try things to know what you are good at. Give it your best, try it out.

AFFIRMATION

I boldly move toward giving my all.

JULY 21

I've been told that I overshare. Sometimes I get criticized for it, but how else would I be if not all of me?

— Bozoma Saint John

This is one woman who shares and gives herself so freely. I admire her boldness to confidently show up in her fullness. I hope that you choose to do the same.

AFFIRMATION

I will nourish my whole self.

JULY 22

Stop letting people who do so little for you control so much of your life.

— **Will Smith**

Regardless of what you do, it's impossible to please everyone, so why keep trying? People pleasing shouldn't be on your priority list.

AFFIRMATION

I won't allow others' thoughts of me affect how I navigate throughout life.

JULY 23

> *I don't think dreams die – I think that people give up.*
>
> — **Tyler Perry**

Don't give up. You deserve to do that thing that makes your heart sing. Take that first step or get back on track to make it happen.

AFFIRMATION

Today, I take one step toward achieving my ultimate dream.

JULY 24

Many people don't focus enough on execution. If you make a commitment to get something done, you need to follow through on that commitment.

— **Kenneth Chenault**

Speed bumps and roadblocks are usually the reasons we give up. There is no problem that doesn't have a solution. You can figure it out or use your tribe to assist you. A commitment to yourself is still a commitment. Make good on your promise to yourself.

AFFIRMATION

I pledge to honor the commitments I make.

JULY 25

You are stronger than you think you are.

— **Leigh Meriweather Knight**

You have underlying strength that you haven't experienced. It will be present when you need it, believe that.

AFFIRMATION

I have the strength to overcome any challenges that come my way.

JULY 26

I thrive on obstacles. If I'm told that it can't be done, then I push harder.

— Issa Rae

Take that obstacle (in my Issa voice)! Go ahead and gut punch those barriers in front of you.

AFFIRMATION

I believe in my strength to push through any obstacle.

JULY 27

Never lookin' back or too far in front of me; the present is a gift, and I just wanna be.

— Common

Seize the second. The present is the present you should be enjoying.

AFFIRMATION

Everything I need will come to me in perfect timing. Now, I'm enjoying this perfect moment.

JULY 28

If you're looking for immediate rewards, you're only looking for the money.

— Eartha Kitt

Chase the passion and the gratitude of fulfillment. The money will always come when you work from a solid, purposeful mission.

AFFIRMATION

I will not use money to measure my wealth.

JULY 29

Know what your target is, don't guess it...if you don't know what your targets are, you're never going to get there.

— Idris Elba

Bullseye! Turn on your tunnel vision and focus on the task at hand.

AFFIRMATION

I have clarity on my assignment.

JULY 30

Anger cancels good judgement!

— **Sister Souljah**

In the heat of the moment, it's easy to say or do something you'll later regret. We've all been there. The best thing we can do is retreat until we get to a place of calmness to handle the matter in a loving and productive manner.

AFFIRMATION

I will take the time I need to process and express my feelings clearly.

JULY 31

I've worked harder and had less.

— **Kimm White**

Hard work is always worth it. You may not achieve what you thought you wanted, but in the long run, you will gain priceless lessons along the way that are far more important than the win itself. Your victory has already been won.

AFFIRMATION

I will continue to stay consistent. It's going to pay off.

AUGUST 1

Some of the ability to reflect on what I really want comes from pushing up against a society that shames me for not having the expected trappings. I'm very pleased with my existence these days. Have I had to learn to make friends with loneliness? Yes. I think if I were in a relationship, it would be the same.

— Tracee Ellis Ross

Self-care and me-time should be mandatory norms in life. We make time for others naturally but neglect our own.

AFFIRMATION

Today, I will do something for ME that brings great vibes to my heart.

AUGUST 2

I don't like to gamble, but if there's one thing I'm willing to bet on, it's myself.

— Beyoncé

Your safest bet and investment is yourself. Gamble it all on you.

AFFIRMATION

Every day, I am moving towards my best life by investing in myself.

AUGUST 3

You've got to say no to the things that don't honor you. No to the things that don't bring you joy. And you don't have to explain your no.

— Iyanla Vanzant

No can be the most powerful word in your vocabulary. Use it. Iyanla has referenced how some people will choose familiar suffering over unknown happiness.

AFFIRMATION

I surrender to needed changes in my life to experience overwhelming joy.

AUGUST 4

It's important for us to also understand that the phrase 'Black Lives Matter' simply refers to the notion that there's a specific vulnerability for African Americans that needs to be addressed. It's not meant to suggest that other lives don't matter. It's to suggest that other folks aren't experiencing this particular vulnerability.

— **President Barack Obama**

Find your inner voice and speak nourishment into your life. We need EVERYONE in this movement because it's NOT a moment. Let's end racial injustice.

AFFIRMATION

Black Lives Matter! Amplify Melanated Voices Everywhere!

AUGUST 5

Life is a motherfucker! I embrace every chapter of it with full acceptance.

— Ashley Adana

The journey called life is a book full of chapters. Chapters of happiness, pain, adventures, disappointments, and so much more. But how blessed are we to live it, to have a chance to share ourselves with others. Live it up my friend!

AFFIRMATION

I'm equipped for all challenges and opportunities that come my way.

AUGUST 6

The only thing stopping you from achieving your dreams are the stories you keep telling yourself that you can't. Don't wait - act now. Regret nothing.

— Denzel Washington

The lies, the lies.... that's what they are. Stop talking down to yourself. Start visualizing what goodness you will receive from taking the risk.

AFFIRMATION

I'm aware of my desires, and I will not wait to pursue them.

AUGUST 7

Love takes off the masks that we fear we cannot live without and know we cannot live within.

— **James Baldwin**

Love is freedom to be your authentic self at all times. What a beautiful space to live within, right?

AFFIRMATION

I am loved.

AUGUST 8

Make sure your desire to do what you're aspiring to do is deeper than just fame and being a celebrity.

— Meagan Good

Let your work be filled with impact and purpose. Notoriety may be a part of it, but don't let it lead the way.

AFFIRMATION

I am completely energized by the work I do.

AUGUST 9

Sometimes it takes a release to soar.

— **Deion Sanders**

We hold on to things based on fear of the unknown or the next thing that will fill that space. The strength is in the release.

AFFIRMATION

I release all things and situations that are stopping my growth.

AUGUST 10

We all get distracted, the question is, would you bounce back or bounce backwards?

— Kendrick Lamar

Stumble, by stumbling forward.

AFFIRMATION

My setbacks make me stronger.

AUGUST 11

I don't have any time to stay up all night worrying about what someone who doesn't love me has to say about me.

— Viola Davis

You need your beauty rest to conquer tomorrow.
Don't let others' opinions consume your space.

AFFIRMATION

I'm breaking the habit of allowing others'
voices to affect my soul and mind.

AUGUST 12

Nobody is as powerful as we make them out to be.

— **Alice Walker**

We are all doing the same thing, experiencing life. We are in the same game, just on different levels. We all encounter pain and pleasure as the next man or woman.

AFFIRMATION

I will enjoy my journey, as it is uniquely designed just for me.

AUGUST 13

There have been so many people who have said to me, 'You can't do that,' but I've had an innate belief that they were wrong. Be unwavering and relentless in your approach.

— **Halle Berry**

Others' thoughts and opinions belong to them. They aren't yours to carry. You have a race to run; stay focused on your own mission.

AFFIRMATION

I am well equipped to reach my goals.

AUGUST 14

Talent is never enough. With few exceptions, the best players are the hardest workers.

— Magic Johnson

Talent is never enough to be successful. It's a good starting point, but you will need things like effort, discipline, drive, persistence, willpower, commitment; the list goes on. Never rely on your natural talent alone.

AFFIRMATION

Hard work pays off, and I am fully committed.

AUGUST 15

We got turned down, we failed, had setbacks, had to start over a lot of times. But we kept going at it. In anybody's case, that's always the distinguishing factor.

— **Nipsey Hussle**

This is a personal favorite of mine. The appreciation level is heightened when more work goes into obtaining a goal.

AFFIRMATION

I have seen and conquered too much to compromise now.

AUGUST 16

I'm a strong black woman, and I cannot be intimidated. I cannot be undermined.

— Maxine Waters

Stand in your power. Your power is in your melanin, in your voice, in your presence.

AFFIRMATION

I'm allowed to shine and take up space.

AUGUST 17

I'm ready for challenges and opportunities that come my way. I'm equipped.

— **Ashley Adana**

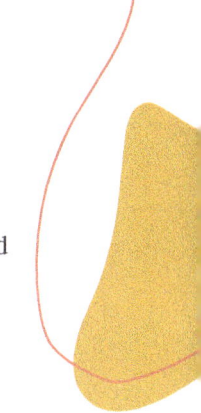

This is a saying I repeat daily. Feel free to add it to your stockpile of positivity.

AFFIRMATION

I am equipped for what's next.

AUGUST 18

Forgiveness is not an occasional act; it is a constant attitude.

— **Martin L. King Jr.**

This is so true. When I read this, I think about forgiving myself. We really give it to ourselves sometimes, right? We play the blame game or have self-pity parties. Sitting in these negative thoughts hold us back from the joy we should be exposed to. So, be gentle with yourself and forgive yourself for the self-inflicted pain you caused.

AFFIRMATION

I will be gentle with myself.

AUGUST 19

Needing nothing attracts everything.

— Russell Simmons

Everything you need is already present. That thought alone will attract your desires. Lead with gratitude. Relax and enjoy your present life. Everything will come in perfect timing.

AFFIRMATION

I don't need anything that I don't have.

AUGUST 20

Women make up more than half of the world's population and potential. So it is neither just nor practical for their voices, for our voices, to go unheard at the highest levels of decision-making.

— **Meghan Markle, Duchess of Sussex**

I raise my glass (cup of coffee) to my sisters and brothers who adjust the crowns of others. Today, pick up the phone and offer one of your sisters encouragement and empowerment to conquer the day. Women, we have to keep doing good with the platforms we are given and the ones we create.

AFFIRMATION

My footprints are not etched in the sand, they are etched in concrete.

AUGUST 21

I decided long ago never to walk in anyone's shadow; if I fail, if I succeed, at least I'll live as I believe.

— Whitney Houston

Go toward your light, your truth. You never have to fade into someone else's background.

AFFIRMATION

I trust in my ability to contribute.

AUGUST 22

It doesn't matter who you are, where you came from. The ability to triumph begins with you. Always.

— Oprah Winfrey

The daily duty you have to yourself is simply to be yourself. You don't have to strive for perfection, love where you are now. Loving your present is the quickest way to create a better future.

AFFIRMATION

I appreciate my journey.

AUGUST 23

I'm reflective only in the sense that I learn to move forward. I reflect with a purpose.

— **Kobe Bryant**

There's a reason the rearview mirror is smaller than the windshield. The road ahead is more important than the road you've already traveled.

AFFIRMATION

My future matters more than my past.

AUGUST 24

We have to find new ways to work without permission, new ways to turn corners and go through doors that are closed off to us to create our own audiences and our own material independently.

— Ava DuVernay

Don't be afraid to do the work alone. You may be the one called to pave the way for others to follow.

AFFIRMATION

I face challenges head on.

AUGUST 25

Opportunities are seldom perfect, but if one is not ready for them, they may not ever come again.

— Dr. Edward Lockhart III

Opportunity favors the prepared.
Prepare your mind. Feed your mind
with new knowledge, new inspirations,
new possibilities and new motivations.

AFFIRMATION

I'm ready for opportunities that come my way.

AUGUST 26

I do a lot of reading, meditating, and praying to stay as grounded as I can be in this crazy world.

— Jada Pinkett Smith

Today is a day for you to do things that make your heart sing. No excuses, today is your day!

AFFIRMATION

Today, I will do things to keep me grounded and bring me joy.

AUGUST 27

I always wanted to be somebody. If I made it, it's half because I was game enough to take a lot of punishment along the way and half because there were a lot of people who cared enough to help me.

— **Althea Gibson**

You will leave any battle with bruises; physical or mental. Your supportive tribe will be there to nurse you back to health so you can journey on.

AFFIRMATION

I am willing to risk it all for my ultimate win.

AUGUST 28

I love to see a young girl go out and grab the world by the lapels. Life's a bitch. You've got to go out and kick ass.

— Maya Angelou

Sometimes, you have to scream out loud, "Watch out world, I have my cape on. I'm about to cause BIG hell around here!"

AFFIRMATION

I will not be distracted today. I've got shit to do.

AUGUST 29

To sit on an idea or fail to act on a goal is not really goal-setting, but wishful thinking.

— **Les Brown**

No room for wishing and hoping when you can just act. The only thing stopping you is you.

AFFIRMATION

Today, I will take action on my goals.

AUGUST 30

You can tell the truth, but sometimes, you can't always be in your face with it. I found a way to tell the truth and put it in a nice, neat package for people to receive it. A lot of times, you have to put it in a nice, neat box with a bow tie, and when they open it, it's the truth. I think people respect that.

— **Shannon Sharpe**

I think we've all been in the boat when emotions led the way, I know I certainly have. The message can be delivered with purpose and authenticity, but if tact is lacking, some may find it harder to hear.

AFFIRMATION

I will stop and repackage my approach for the message I need others to receive.

AUGUST 31

Trust yourself. Think for yourself. Act for yourself. Speak for yourself. Be yourself. Imitation is suicide.

— **Marva Collins**

Yes and yes - it's a reminder that you hold a shit load of value. Trust in your abilities and feed yourself new knowledge to grow beyond your present.

AFFIRMATION

The world wouldn't be the same without me.

SEPTEMBER 1

Never compromise who you are personally to become who you wish to be professionally.

— **Janice Bryant Howroyd**

Staying true to your beliefs, your motives, and your truths will take you where you should be in all facets of life.

AFFIRMATION

I will only give my true self to the world.

SEPTEMBER 2

Everything is worth it. The hard work, the times when you're tired, the times where you're a bit sad, in the end, it's all worth it because it really makes me happy. There's nothing better than loving what you do.

— Aaliyah Haughton

You are entitled to live a life of your own choosing. If you are willing to go periods of time sacrificing comforts, you can get the happiness you are seeking.

AFFIRMATION

I'm ready to make my dreams my reality.

SEPTEMBER 3

If you prioritize yourself, you are going to save yourself.

— Gabrielle Union

Make time to feed your soul goodness. It's not indulgence, it's self-preservation.

AFFIRMATION

Happiness is an inside job.

SEPTEMBER 4

Be present, be intentional with your actions, focus on the now and you'll be at peace.

— Dominique Dolyce

Let tomorrow worry about itself, today is the one that counts.

AFFIRMATION

I'm in charge of how I feel, and today I'm choosing peace.

SEPTEMBER 5

Each day, awake and let God speak into your life. His word cannot return void.

— Anthony Miller

The most precious and intimate relationship I have is with God. I'm blessed to hear his voice. He will speak to you in an unmistakably way that it touches your heart. How do you know it's God? The message will align with his teachings. Recognize that God communicates in many forms, but most often it's through your mind and heart.

AFFIRMATION

Allow me to meet and receive the messages in front of me with full acceptance.

SEPTEMBER 6

Look whoever you're talking to in the eyes. Don't look away. Two reasons: you can tell whether they are lying. Also, so that they can see whatever you're saying you mean and you can connect to that person.

— **Idris Elba**

Hold your head up, look them in the eyes, open your ears, then listen to your heart. This combination is where the truth lives.

AFFIRMATION

I am trustworthy, and I give others the opportunity to display the same trait.

SEPTEMBER 7

I decided in my life that I would do nothing that did not reflect positively on my father's life.

— Sidney Poitier

Let your pride from your ancestors guide your decisions. You will want the generations behind you to admire your legacy. There is a saying, "As you do for your ancestors, your children will do for you."

AFFIRMATION

I honor my last name and my DNA.

SEPTEMBER 8

I'm in a position that allows me to do what I want to do, and I do it.

— **Eddie Murphy**

Now, that's some freedom. Get clear on what you want your life to look like, then take the necessary steps without hesitation. You are the writer of your life, you call the shots. Every decision you make affects your tomorrow. Choose wisely; your future depends on it.

AFFIRMATION

I am responsible for the life I desire.

SEPTEMBER 9

Tolerance, compromise, understanding, acceptance, patience - I want those all to be very sharp tools in my shed.

— CeeLo Green

Those are great tools to have. I would add faith, drive, positive thoughts, freedom, and compassion for a solid top 10. Write down your top 10 and say them daily. You will notice the change in your life.

AFFIRMATION

My life toolbox will bring me success.

SEPTEMBER 10

Embrace compassion and kindness. Give good energy to expect good energy.

— **LaShonda Dixon**

You have the choice to spread goodness in the world. When you give goodness to others is when you receive happiness. Someone will give it to you too, just keep doing your part.

AFFIRMATION

I will give the world good vibes today.

SEPTEMBER 11

At the end of the day, I stand by who I am. I'm a good person.

— **Taraji P. Henson**

If your reflection in the mirror feels good in your soul, you are good.

AFFIRMATION

I am in love with who I am and who I'm becoming.

SEPTEMBER 12

When all you have are unanswered questions about life, God waits for the opportunity to provide the answer you need!

— Roderick Benson

He's an on-time God. When you get weary, he is right there to help you over the hurdle, so you can be on your merry way. But we have to remember, it's in his time. He has provided us the tools to weather the storm. You got this. Hold on.

AFFIRMATION

I trust God's timing for me.

SEPTEMBER 13

Comparison is an act of violence against the self.

— Iyanla Vanzant

I can guarantee you one thing, no one can do you better than you! Your journey is as unique as you are. Embrace that.

AFFIRMATION

I am kind to myself and my development.

SEPTEMBER 14

My peace is from the Spirit within, and it cannot be taken away. It's mine!

— **D'Etta Sumlin**

You have to acknowledge the source of your peace. It's bigger than you alone. There is a higher power that gives you protection to sit in your harmonious peace.

AFFIRMATION

I recognize my peace provider.

SEPTEMBER 15

Follow your heart.

— **Keisha Wilson**

What are you waiting for? Allow
your heart to nudge you in the right
direction. Acknowledge those subtle
encouragments your heart is giving you.

AFFIRMATION

I will allow my heart to lead the way.

SEPTEMBER 16

The way I was raised, you listen to people. You don't tell them who they are, you let them tell you.

— Tamron Hall

Give others the opportunity to show up in their wholeness as you would desire for yourself. Now, when they show us, you still have a choice if you want them in your space, as they have the same choice.

AFFIRMATION

I appreciate others for who they are.

SEPTEMBER 17

Success is talent plus preparation.

— **Malcolm Gladwell**

Success is a learnable skill that takes commitment and practice. When you decide to put the effort into your desired results, you can win.

AFFIRMATION

It doesn't matter where I am right now, I'm preparing for greater.

SEPTEMBER 18

I don't have to go around trying to save everybody anymore; that's not my job.

— Jada Pinkett Smith

As women, we are natural nurturers. We will take on the load of our loved ones in the name of love. Know that those loads can get heavy on your shoulders. Your duty isn't to carry others' burdens.

AFFIRMATION

The responsibility to myself is myself.

SEPTEMBER 19

> *The battles that count aren't the ones for gold medals. The struggles within yourself—the invisible, inevitable battles inside all of us—that's where it's at.*
>
> — Jesse Owens

That inner enemy is something else, right? You are not alone. We all have struggles we are trying to conquer daily. The victory can be yours as long as you keep trying. Life isn't perfect, and think of all you have overcome previously. Keep pushing. Don't burn yourself out focusing on the uncontrollables life gives you.

AFFIRMATION

This is my life and I'm in charge.

SEPTEMBER 20

I realized I was more convincing to myself and to the people who were listening when I actually said what I thought, versus what I thought people wanted to hear me say.

— Ursula Burns

This one really touched home for me. As I was writing this book, I went back and forth about adding my own thoughts with each quote and affirmation. Why? Because sometimes I think, who wants to hear my opinions? But my voice is worthy and authentically mine. Those who want to hear it will listen and be inspired. I hope you are.

AFFIRMATION

My authenticity is enough.

SEPTEMBER 21

I don't in any way disparage any time I've had in the trenches because it really has made me the artist I am today.

— Billy Porter

Character is built through time and experiences. What you choose to do with both will be the definition of your legacy.

AFFIRMATION

I'm grateful for every lesson of life.

SEPTEMBER 22

Your career is what you're paid for.
Your calling is what you're made for.

— Steve Harvey

You work to pay the bills, but how you serve is your calling. Both are necessary to survive. Whenever we do something that fills us with enthusiasm and is pleasing to God, that's when you are fulfilling your calling.

AFFIRMATION

I will stay true to my calling.

SEPTEMBER 23

If they are toxic, they're toxic. Your love for them doesn't change that.

— **Ashley Adana**

Characteristics of toxic people: they are negative, they always criticize your decisions, they don't care, they waste your time, they keep disappointing you, they are manipulative, they always play the victim. Ok, you get my drift. Our tolerance for toxicity is totally dependent on the person and relationship, and only you can decide when someone needs to be removed from your life.

AFFIRMATION

I am free to let go of anyone that no longer serves me goodness.

SEPTEMBER 24

If we give our children sound self-love, they will be able to deal with whatever life puts before them.

— Bell Hooks

Give the little ones in your life room to be. Give them a chance to speak their truth. You are giving them tools that will last a lifetime.

AFFIRMATION

I will allow the little ones in my life to boldly be themselves.

SEPTEMBER 25

Money and success don't change people; they merely amplify what is already there.

— Will Smith

Be the person you desire to be right now; no use in waiting.

AFFIRMATION

I will work to become who I want to be now.

SEPTEMBER 26

I am lucky that whatever fear I have inside me, my desire to win is always stronger.

— **Serena Williams**

That burning fire in your soul, hold onto it stronger than the misery that comes with fear.

AFFIRMATION

Today, my desire to win will shine bright.

SEPTEMBER 27

As long as we are not ourselves, we will try to be what other people are.

— Malidoma Patrice Somé

Don't do it, don't compare. You don't know their story, focus on yours. They have their own shit going on, trust.

AFFIRMATION

I approve of myself and love myself deeply.

SEPTEMBER 28

If I ever consider myself underneath someone, it's simply because I'm there lifting them up.

— Stacey Tripp

Perception is key. Helping your tribe excel is a blessing. Give them the support they need, yours will be there when you need it too.

AFFIRMATION

It's a privilege to uplift others.

SEPTEMBER 29

Don't settle for average. Bring your best to the moment. Then, whether it fails or succeeds, at least you know you gave all you had. We need to live the best that's in us.

— **Angela Bassett**

You've got to think high to rise. You have to expect more from yourself to thrive. Give it your best.

AFFIRMATION

I will be rewarded because of the effort I give.

SEPTEMBER 30

All I know is who I am. At the end of the day, all I know is my intentions, and no matter what you take out of context, no matter what pictures you post, I know what I am aligned with. I know what my truth is.

— **Issa Rae**

As long as you know what your intentions are, that's all that counts. What others have to say is just their opinion. It doesn't hold weight in your world.

AFFIRMATION

I cannot control the narrative others feel about me, as I don't have a desire to.

OCTOBER 1

No idea is original, there's nothing new under the sun, it's never what you do, but how it's done.

— Nasir Jones

It's no need in wasting a lot of time trying to reinvent the wheel. Use the time to make the wheel your own. Yes, it already exists, but it needs your talents and touch on it. Go for it.

AFFIRMATION

I am open to the magic that I can bring to life in my own way.

OCTOBER 2

So no matter how hard it gets, stick your chest out, keep ya head up…. and handle it.

— **Tupac Shakur**

This is life; it's unpredictable. Sometimes things don't make sense and shit happens. Raise your head and keep on going.

AFFIRMATION

I will not give up because I have not exhausted all possibilities.

OCTOBER 3

Stop lookin' at what you ain't got, and start being thankful for what you do got.

— T.I. Harris

Wake up each day with gratitude. It's a reminder of how blessed you really are.

AFFIRMATION

I am so blessed for everything I have.

OCTOBER 4

If you wake up deciding what you want to give versus what you're going to get, you become a more successful person.

— **Russell Simmons**

Money isn't the only form of currency you can give. You can give your time, your love, your possessions.

AFFIRMATION

I give freely without expectations.

OCTOBER 5

We're capable of so much more than we allow ourselves to believe.

— Queen Latifah

Believe you have more inside of you.

AFFIRMATION

I'm stepping outside of my comfort to become the greatest version of myself.

OCTOBER 6

I feel sorry for anybody that could let hate wrap them up. Ain't no such thing as I can hate anybody and hope to see God's face.

— Fannie Lou Hamer

Hate is a strong word and a heavier emotion. Don't bear the weight.

AFFIRMATION

Hate has no place in my life.

OCTOBER 7

I never want to feel too far away from people. I think that's when you get in trouble.

— Lena Waithe

Embrace your blackness, your people, your ancestors, your family. Live in the greatness you were blessed with.

AFFIRMATION

I am in touch and in tune with my people.

OCTOBER 8

The only justification for ever looking down on somebody is to pick them up.

— Jesse Jackson

Don't look down on others with judgement. You are here to be an example by displaying compassion and understanding. Looking down on others is a dangerous game to partake in, because that may be the very person you look up to tomorrow.

AFFIRMATION

I will not pass judgment on others.

OCTOBER 9

If I cannot do great things, I can do small things in a great way.

— Martin L. King Jr.

All contributions to the greater good count.

AFFIRMATION

I am a seed, able to produce special fruits.

OCTOBER 10

We obviously feel destiny and purpose and do what we do, but within that are ways to help others and to inspire others and to support and encourage people.

— Common

Helping others is a lifetime duty that we should always take pride in. When we hold up to our end, those we touch will be inspired to do the same.

AFFIRMATION

I will be a light for myself and those I surround myself with.

OCTOBER 11

You are on the eve of a complete victory. You can't go wrong. The world is behind you.

— Josephine Baker

You can. You will. End of story.

AFFIRMATION

I am victorious.

OCTOBER 12

There is reasoning behind every challenge in life. They're never to break you but strengthen you.

— Sharon Bolden

One interesting thing about stress is that we often only view it as negative. It's our attitude toward stress that has to shift. Nooooow, I'm not saying that stress isn't stressful. If you think "okay, game on!" rather than "game over," you can tackle it differently.

AFFIRMATION

I gain strength from my challenges.

OCTOBER 13

Normally I don't tell people about the projects that I want to do. Some people have a tendency to be like "ah, you should do this" or discourage you from doing it, and I would get in my own head.

— Issa Rae

Sharing is not always caring. It's ok to just show up with that new haircut or start your own business without input. You are the writer in this story and a proofreader isn't necessary.

AFFIRMATION

Others' opinions and plans for my life are void.

OCTOBER 14

Honesty, trust, and friendship in a relationship are crucial, and no relationship can survive without them.

— Hill Harper

I love these. I would add communication to the list too. The priceless feeling of having a partner who gives you freedom to speak your truth, express your opinions, and share your aspirations.... that's good stuff. Require these things as they are due to you.

AFFIRMATION

I'm grateful to have a partner that honors my entire being.

OCTOBER 15

There is a child in all of us, a person who believes in a glorious future.

— Jasmine Guy

Your possibilities are endless. Dig deep and allow your little ambitious self to come up to speak life into you today.

AFFIRMATION

My life is as bright as the sun and as big as the ocean.

OCTOBER 16

I'm tryna learn something new. I'm tryna surround myself with people that inspire me or at least inquire similar desires.

— Kendrick Lamar

Elevation Extensions. This is what I call people in my inner circle who inspire me to do more and reach new heights.

AFFIRMATION

My tribe expects more of me. I appreciate that.

OCTOBER 17

Never be limited by other people's limited imaginations.

— Mae Jemison

Everyone you meet won't see your magic.
That's ok as long as you do. Abracadabra!

AFFIRMATION

I'm focused. I've got my eye on the prize.

OCTOBER 18

Procrastination will delay your change! Today is a very good day to change; don't let you stop yourself from growing.

— **Steve Harvey**

Hesitation has no place here. We procrastinate for a few reasons: because we want things to truly remain, we are protecting our ego from being hurt, or we're just being lazy. Every day is a new day to take a stab at it. Start today.

AFFIRMATION

I'm going to make the most out of today. My future depends on it.

OCTOBER 19

My work is like my vacation, so in a way every day is like Saturday.

— Ludacris

I love this! Saturday every day. Don't create a life where you live for the weekend. The week is too long to only enjoy two days. Start recreating your life if needed.

AFFIRMATION

I don't have to escape my reality, I love the life I have designed.

OCTOBER 20

I was raised to be an independent woman, not the victim of anything.

— **Kamala Harris**

I was raised the same way. Pity parties have to be short lived. Allow yourself a chance to process those hurtful feelings and get on with it. Harboring negative emotions only hold you down, not the person or thing that inflicted the pain.

AFFIRMATION

I'm a survivor, not a victim.

OCTOBER 21

Don't let your inability to do everything undermine your determination to do something.

— Cory Booker

Love this! You can learn along the way. Go for it.

AFFIRMATION

I am determined to take action today.

OCTOBER 22

I've planned, researched, talked about it. Enough is enough. It's time for me to start doing.

— **Ashley Adana**

Listen, I will research the hell out of some stuff. I will research myself right out of a brilliant idea. You know what that's called, right? Fear, fear of the unknown. I've learned to view it differently. I now look at it as excitement for the possibility, the new opportunities that can come from it, the lives I can touch with my work. It's all about the shift in your mindset.

AFFIRMATION

Implementation is the goal.

OCTOBER 23

I believe in a God of a second chance and a God of love and mercy, because I need so much more of it myself.

— Michael Eric Dyson

Thank you, thank you.

AFFIRMATION

Thank you, Lord, for all of your forgiveness;
past, present and future.

OCTOBER 24

I wouldn't change a single thing, because one change alters every moment that follows it.

— Sidney Poitier

So true. Honor the stripes you've received along the way. It's all part of your beauty.

AFFIRMATION

I am thankful for my journey, as is.

OCTOBER 25

I truly believe that if you put your goals in writing, speak them out loud, and work for them, they will happen.

— Ciara

This is exactly why I wrote this book. It's for others to be encouraged to speak new life into themselves. When we believe it, speak it, write it, we have no choice but to see it come to life.

AFFIRMATION

Whatever I seek to achieve, I will receive.

OCTOBER 26

Each and every one of you has the power, the will and the capacity to make a difference in the world in which you live in.

— **Harry Belafonte**

Start in your own home, your own neighborhood, your business, your city, and then travel further. Leave your sprinkles of goodness wherever you go.

AFFIRMATION

Today, I will make a difference in my world.

OCTOBER 27

The greatest gift is not being afraid to question.

— Ruby Dee

Asking questions is a way to get closer to clarity. I'm a who, what, when, how, and why type of girl. I'm naturally inquisitive. Ask away. It's a golden opportunity to learn and possibly avoid unforeseen hazards.

AFFIRMATION

I will ask questions to receive a deeper understanding.

OCTOBER 28

If someone lacked decency or respect, I didn't allow that person to stay in my world.

— **Gabrielle Union**

If you don't vibe, you don't vibe. You don't have to force it.

AFFIRMATION

I value my tribe.

OCTOBER 29

Take what you like and leave the rest.

— **Tracee Ellis Ross**

You get to accept and embrace the things that feel good to you.

AFFIRMATION

I reject all those things that don't sit well with my soul.

OCTOBER 30

There can be no progress/achievement without sacrifice.

— **Frankie Williams, Sr.**

Sacrifices can be hard but also rewarding. When you make a choice to give up something you treasure, you can only hope that what's received is something of more value.

AFFIRMATION

I am willing to go without in some areas to gain in others.

OCTOBER 31

When someone shows you who they are, believe them the first time.

— Maya Angelou

It's so important to believe what a person demonstrates themselves to be, regardless of who they claim they are or who we desire them to be.

AFFIRMATION

I will accept the face value of others, not the value I stamped on them.

NOVEMBER 1

I prayed to the Lord and he answered me, freeing me from my fears!

— Jamie Fuller

Have you ever been so frightened, you think your heart is going to jump out of your chest? Heaviness in your throat? Understand that it's fear and it will pass. One way to help it pass is by knowing you have a source that is there to walk you through it. Stop, be still, take a few deep breaths then pray.

AFFIRMATION

Nothing can stand in my way.

NOVEMBER 2

> *Sometimes we try to hold on to the very things that God himself is trying to tear apart.*
>
> — Tyler Perry

You can attract all the things meant for you if you stop resisting the release of the things that aren't for you. We have to sometimes release our own agenda and accept spiritual guidance. Constant friction isn't a part of the life God desires for us. We have to release that stuff. We must trust that there's a plan far beyond our own understanding and just surrender. Surrender in the name of future love and joy.

AFFIRMATION

I'm willing to release what's not for me to attract more of what's meant for me.

NOVEMBER 3

It is important to surround yourself with people who lift you up, encourage you, share your vision and inspire you.

— **Les Brown**

Send an email or text to your top 5 supporters. Let them know you appreciate their presence. Love on your people.

AFFIRMATION

I will show gratitude to my support tribe.

NOVEMBER 4

It always seems impossible until it's done.

— Sean "Diddy" Combs

Damn right! The struggle to get to the finish line can seem like a long one. And sometimes it is because we can't always sprint through life. Some things require a marathon. Another thing, don't strive for perfection, completion should be the goal.

AFFIRMATION

I will endure to meet the victory.

NOVEMBER 5

You can't be hesitant about who you are.

— **Viola Davis**

Accept your beauty, strengths, weaknesses, imperfections, and every other part that creates the wholeness that is you. You are a badass in all of your uniqueness. Embrace that.

AFFIRMATION

I love all of me, as is.

NOVEMBER 6

I'm committed to starting over.

— Iyanla Vanzant

Sometimes you have to erase it all. Clean house. It's ok to flip that page and start a new chapter.

AFFIRMATION

I genuinely celebrate my new beginning.

NOVEMBER 7

I cannot control anything. This is the most powerful fact when we accept the gift of God through His only begotten Son. Then trying becomes trusting, even in "pandemics." Running becomes resting. Wondering becomes prayer, and therein, we find strength and peace for each day - one at a time.

— Jean Lovett

This is such a powerful statement. Read it again, out loud. Now, let it sit in your spirit.

AFFIRMATION

I rest well in the arms of the Lord.

NOVEMBER 8

I am not getting any younger and am taking a new approach to life.

— Alfre Woodard

Your age should never be a reason for you to stop setting new goals for yourself. You still have offerings to give to the world and blessings to receive.

AFFIRMATION

I can start something, right now.

NOVEMBER 9

We know that when a woman speaks truth to power, there will be attempts to put her down... I'm not going to go anywhere.

— Maxine Waters

Stand your ground. You have space around you that needs to be filled. Take it up.

AFFIRMATION

I am allowed to exist as I am.

NOVEMBER 10

If you stop and think about what you are about to say or do, you might not say or do it.

— Myderia Miller-Tripp

Impulsive and impatient moments. Honey, I've had many of these. I stop and tell myself, "Look before you leap, Ashley." I will always phone a friend if needed to process my emotions or create my action plan. That's what friends are for, right? Help bring me back to Earth, girlfriend.

AFFIRMATION

I will take the time needed to clear my mind before I move forward.

NOVEMBER 11

I'm about seeing long-term, seeing a vision, understanding nothing really worthwhile happens overnight, and just sticking to your script long enough to make something real happen.

— Nipsey Hussle

The key to winning a marathon is finding the sweet spot to endure the distance. Consistently pouring into your plan will get you to the finish line.

AFFIRMATION

I'm committed to the marathon, the long-distance race.

NOVEMBER 12

We all have self-doubt. You don't deny it, but you also don't capitulate to it. You embrace it.

— Kobe Bryant

There are some days when doubt seems to speak a little louder than confidence. It's totally normal to encounter. We can embrace it, just don't let it paralyze you. Process and proceed.

AFFIRMATION

I'm not perfect, I'm just human.

NOVEMBER 13

It's being willing to walk away that gives you strength and power - if you're willing to accept the consequences of doing what you want to do.

— Whoopi Goldberg

There's a season for everything. Release is a part of it too. Difficult circumstances come, but they go too.

AFFIRMATION

All things work together for my ultimate good.

NOVEMBER 14

If you want to be successful, you have to be willing to use every connection you've got.

— Magic Johnson

Your network is your net worth. Your rolodex can take you to the next level, so beware of where you spend your time.

AFFIRMATION

I trust in my abilities and my network to lift me to the next level.

NOVEMBER 15

There is a reason they called it chasing your dreams and not walking after them.

— **Shannon Sharpe**

Lace up those kicks, stretch, and hit the road with a vengeance. You have goals to reach and a legacy to leave.

AFFIRMATION

I will pursue my dreams with fierceness.

NOVEMBER 16

It's okay to be a freak.

— Lisa Bonet

Love it! We all are in some sense of the word, right? Unusual and unexpected. We don't have to conform to the world. Find your tribe that is as freaky as you are.

AFFIRMATION

I embrace the part of myself that others don't understand.

NOVEMBER 17

No action is too small when it comes to changing the world... I'm inspired every time I meet an entrepreneur who is succeeding against all odds.

— Cyril Ramaphosa

Entrepreneur or not, your efforts are making an impact around you. Keep winning against all odds.

AFFIRMATION

I've been chosen to be successful.

NOVEMBER 18

If you want to be successful, you have to jump, there's no way around it. If you're safe, you'll never soar.

— Steve Harvey

You have to jump, sometimes without a parachute. Yes, you will encounter hard times and failures along the way, but those are important too because they help you learn how to do things the right way.

AFFIRMATION

I'm ready to take flight.

NOVEMBER 19

If it doesn't work, you can always try something else.

— **Shonda Glover**

Give it your all and take the shot! You'll always gain a win in some aspect when you at least try. A dear entrepreneur friend told me, "Try it. Eventually you will nail the right thing."

AFFIRMATION

I have the power to do anything I put my mind to.

NOVEMBER 20

Never ever chase money. You should chase success, because with success money follows.

— Wilfred Emmanuel-Jones

Money won't bring you happiness. It's having satisfaction and meaning in your life that will bring joy. When you have a life filled with purposeful work, money and opportunities to make more will flow towards you.

AFFIRMATION

I am grateful for the abundance that I have and the abundance on its way.

NOVEMBER 21

Change will not come if we wait for some other person or some other time. We are the ones we've been waiting for. We are the change that we seek.

— **President Barack Obama**

NO effort or contribution is too small to give.
Your gift gives weight to change.

AFFIRMATION

I will do good things to bring about change for others.

NOVEMBER 22

My biggest dream is to see little black and brown people playing in the sun, splashing in the ocean for generations to come. And know that the power of women will always be waiting at the shores to receive them.

— **Taraji P. Henson**

Wow, this statement is so powerful. Ladies, we are paving the way for the next generation. They will get to see the excellence you shared with the world and know that it's possible for them. Keep shining.

AFFIRMATION

My present will empower the future.

NOVEMBER 23

You never know which experiences of life are going to be of value . . . You've got to leave yourself open to the hidden opportunities.

— **Robin Roberts**

Show up and show out with each opportunity you receive. It's opening doors to others you can't imagine.

AFFIRMATION

I invite the unthinkable opportunities I cannot see.

NOVEMBER 24

Thank you, Lord, for closed doors.

— Ashley Adana

When it's not for you, it is what it is. You don't need it. Let it go.

AFFIRMATION

I'm grateful for everything God has removed.

NOVEMBER 25

We have to not just open our eyes to what's going on in other places; we need to open our eyes to what's going on right in front of us.

— **Forest Whitaker**

Wow, that's powerful. We don't have to go far to examine a lot.

AFFIRMATION

I am observant of my surroundings.

NOVEMBER 26

Sometimes you've got to let everything go – purge yourself. If you are unhappy with anything… whatever is bringing you down, get rid of it. Because you'll find that when you're free, your true creativity, your true self comes out.

— Tina Turner

The closing of one chapter of life, allows for the beauty of the next one to begin.

AFFIRMATION

Today, I will close out a needed chapter in my life.

NOVEMBER 27

No person is your friend who demands your silence, or denies your right to grow.

— **Alice Walker**

If your friends don't rejoice in your wins, call you on your wrongs, hold you to being your best self.... they aren't your people. Get new friends.

AFFIRMATION

I love who I am and attract others who love me too.

NOVEMBER 28

Money had never been the main thing for me. It's the legacy that was important.

— Berry Gordy

Leaving your stamp, that's a true legacy. What will others say about you when you aren't around? Let that lead you.

AFFIRMATION

I am creating a lasting legacy.

NOVEMBER 29

I truly believe in positive synergy, that your positive mindset gives you a more hopeful outlook, and belief that you can do something great means you will do something great.

— Russell Wilson

There is power in your thoughts and words. Be kind to yourself with the words you choose because they will affect your reality.

AFFIRMATION

I only speak goodness in my life.

NOVEMBER 30

You don't make progress by standing on the sidelines, whimpering and complaining. You make progress by implementing ideas.

— **Shirley Chisholm**

The negative thoughts are draining. It's time to become full from the growth you will see. From the things you are going to start implementing.

AFFIRMATION

I'm in charge of the change I want to see in my life.

DECEMBER 1

Embrace what makes you unique, even if it makes others uncomfortable. I didn't have to become perfect because I've learned throughout my journey that perfection is the enemy of greatness.

— Janelle Monae

God created us all uniquely. Get out of your own way and embrace your bomb ass-ness.

AFFIRMATION

I am enough on my own, and my greatness is grand.

DECEMBER 2

Forgiveness is giving up the hope that the past could have been any different. It's accepting the past for what it was, and using this moment and this time to help yourself move forward.

— Oprah Winfrey

Appreciate the past for what it was. You've got more life to live and it needs your full attention.

AFFIRMATION

I believe my future is bright, and that's my focus.

DECEMBER 3

Walk out into the world with a bounce in your step and a song in your heart.

— Russell Simmons

A friendly reminder of how to show up daily.

AFFIRMATION

Today will be a great day.

DECEMBER 4

> *People look at you strange, say you changed. Like you worked that hard to stay the same.*
>
> — Jay-Z

Evolution of self should be a daily exercise. Keep working to be a better person each day you are blessed to be on Earth.

AFFIRMATION

I happily accept my authentic self today.

DECEMBER 5

So many people think being single is the end of something, but it's really a beginning - a good beginning.

— Lauren London

It's so much beauty in being single. It's truly a time to grow and be with yourself on so many levels.

AFFIRMATION

The most important person I will ever love is myself.

DECEMBER 6

There's a time in your life. When you find who you are. That's the golden time of day. And in your mind, you will find you're a bright shining star.

— Frankie Beverly

Shine, Sunshine!

AFFIRMATION

This is my time to shine bright.

DECEMBER 7

I could not have made it this far had there not been angels along the way.

— Della Reese

Thankful for my ancestors, for being a fence around me and speaking in my ear when necessary. You can hear them whispering to you, "Be grateful."

AFFIRMATION

I express gratitude to my ancestors above.

DECEMBER 8

The most alluring thing a woman can have is confidence.

— **Beyoncé**

Let perfectionism go because it won't be fulfilled.

AFFIRMATION

Today, I will work on accepting the greatness that is me.

DECEMBER 9

If you can find something you love, go for it every day of your life, and it would be really good to you.

— Jenifer Lewis

"Just ok" and "love" are different. Go after love, it's more rewarding.

AFFIRMATION

I will work passionately towards things I love.

DECEMBER 10

Success isn't about how much money you make; it's about the difference you make in people's lives.

— Michelle Obama

Impact, Impact, Impact. Touch someone's heart. You can be successful every day with your actions.

AFFIRMATION

I will give more of myself for the benefit of others.

DECEMBER 11

Focused. I'm a hustler. And my hustle is trying to figure out the best ways to do what I like without having to do much else.

— **Yasiin Bey**

Message for the day: laser focus on a lane. Become an expert in one then expand. Hell, expansion may not be the goal either. Being the best in your lane is good enough.

AFFIRMATION

Day by day, I'm becoming the best in my area of expertise.

DECEMBER 12

I hope that there are no persons that would want to think ill of me in any direction or any behavior.

— Diahann Carroll

You can only control your motives, not others' perceptions of you.

AFFIRMATION

I choose to be kind to those I encounter.

DECEMBER 13

You are what you repeatedly do when things get hard.

— Jamie Foxx

Hard times are just that: hard. Don't deny it, acknowledge it. Create an effective plan to deal and cope with hard times. I personally go to heavy mediation and prayer then create my plan. Try not to give much energy to the things you can't control and change those things in your reach.

AFFIRMATION

I'm equipped to handle difficult circumstances.

DECEMBER 14

Your willingness to look at your darkness is what empowers you to change.

— Iyanla Vanzant

Talk about calling you out on your BS with love and truth. Thank you, Ms. Vanzant. From a distance, I have been "checked" several times. Her no nonsense delivery, I love it!

AFFIRMATION

I embrace my flaws, and I am excited about my path of transformation.

DECEMBER 15

I hated every minute of training, but I said, 'Don't quit. Suffer now and live the rest of your life as a champion.'

— Muhammad Ali

Quiet the noise in your head. Envision the full harvest you are going to reap. Now, turn up the volume on the task to achieve your sweet victory.

AFFIRMATION

Quitting isn't an option for me.

DECEMBER 16

Don't leave this world without giving it your all.

— Tupac Shakur

Take today to really think about what you really want in life. Are you working towards it? Are you living a lively life? Are you enjoying your journey? I can guarantee you that you deserve to have the best life you can obtain. Now, you have to work for it, but you damn sure deserve it.

AFFIRMATION

I am working hard to leave an impactful legacy.

DECEMBER 17

If everyone will love one, everyone will be loved.

— **Dr. I.E. Mack**

Have you heard of the 5 love languages? They are the ways people give and receive love. They are: words of affirmation, acts of service, receiving gifts, quality time, and physical touch. Learn your language, learn the language of your inner circle, and start spreading that love around.

AFFIRMATION

Love is the greatest gift that I can give and receive.

DECEMBER 18

Believe in yourself, work hard, work smart and passionately present your best self to the world.

— Hill Harper

Sustaining your motivation can be a hard task sometimes. We all have those days. But we have goals to meet, so get on it.

AFFIRMATION

I offer my best self to the world today and every day afterwards.

DECEMBER 19

Challenges make you discover things about yourself that you never really knew.

— Cicely Tyson

Life is about discovery. Be willing to explore yourself, your community, the world.

AFFIRMATION

I accept the challenges in front of me with full acceptance.

DECEMBER 20

There is no royal flower-strewn path to success. And if there is, I have not found it, for whatever success I have attained has been the result of much hard work and many sleepless nights.

— Madam C.J. Walker

If you are looking for the short cut or the completely paved path to your dreams.... stay asleep lol. Hard work is the answer you will hear from any successful individual. Yep, you've got work to do so get to it.

AFFIRMATION

I am ready to make my dreams a reality by doing the work.

DECEMBER 21

Painters get up and paint. Writers get up and write. I like to get up and act. It's not a big deal. It makes me happy.

— Samuel L. Jackson

Do the things that make your heart sing.
Simple.

AFFIRMATION

My work makes a difference in other people's lives.

DECEMBER 22

The best doctors: rest, sunshine, love, air, purpose-filled career, exercise, friendship, and peace.

— Ashley Adana

Strive to have all of the above and enjoy a good life.

AFFIRMATION

I'm living a blessed life.

DECEMBER 23

Remind yourself daily that vibrations create your life.

— Arianna Johnson

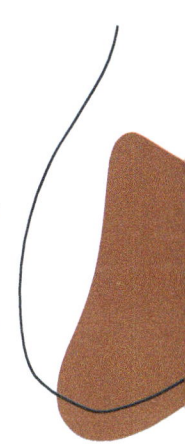

This speaks to the law of attraction, whatever you focus on is what you will attract into your life. You've heard people speak about good or bad vibes, thoughts becoming things, you receive what you believe. These all align with your vibrations. Believe good and receive it.

AFFIRMATION

I am what I believe myself to be. My vibe attracts my tribe.

DECEMBER 24

If you try to follow everyone else's mold, you'll probably fail at some point because God created us uniquely for a reason.

— Queen Latifah

Inspiration and imitation aren't the same. Be inspired to write your own version and put your stamp on.

AFFIRMATION

I will use my talent and skills to create my own unique thing.

DECEMBER 25

Live Courageously.

— **Jillian Smith**

Fierce, fearless, and brave. That's what I wish for you.

AFFIRMATION

I live courageously.

DECEMBER 26

I don't want to be the next Michael Jordan, I only want to be Kobe Bryant.

— **Kobe Bryant**

Nobody else's stats matter, only your last best. No time for scoreboard watching, you have the next shot to take.

AFFIRMATION

I will only compete with myself to be the best version of myself.

DECEMBER 27

I think our life is a journey, and we make mistakes, and it's how we learn from those mistakes and rebound from those mistakes that sets us on the path that we're meant to be on.

— Jay Ellis

Mistakes are necessary. If you are alive, you have made a few. If you keep living, you will make a few more. That's a good thing, it means you are trying.

AFFIRMATION

I am capable of moving beyond my mistakes.

DECEMBER 28

You never know how or when you'll have an impact, or how important your example can be to someone else.

— **Denzel Washington**

Be your genuine self, live in your own happiness, and share your best self with the world. People are inspired by your movement and you don't even know it.

AFFIRMATION

I'll do my best to be the light for others by shining for myself.

DECEMBER 29

I've viewed myself as slightly above average in talent. And where I excel is ridiculous, sickening work ethic.

— Will Smith

Most of us have talent, but it's what we do with it that sets our lives apart from others.

AFFIRMATION

My work ethic will super exceed my talent.

DECEMBER 30

I am willing to compromise. I am not willing to be compromised.

— Myderia Miller-Tripp

Your obligation isn't to adjust yourself but adjust the atmosphere. It's important that you be yourself at all times.

AFFIRMATION

I am one of a kind.

DECEMBER 31

I think everybody at some point - especially if they've been working their whole lives - should take time out and think about what they've done.

— **Gregory Hines**

I totally agree. One thing I like to do at the end of the year is take time to go through my social media pages or camera roll. It allows me to appreciate the rollercoaster that was the last 365 days of my life. Cheers to a new year and new adventures, my friend.

AFFIRMATION

I'm grateful for the last 365 days I've been blessed to experience.

About Ashley

She's a sassy-mouthed Georgia peach who loves the Lord and uses a healthy number of expressive F-bombs to drive points home. This Leo Lioness is a yoga enthusiast, who practices often, with dreams of attending a retreat in Thailand or Morocco (soon). She is the straight-talk girlfriend with a strong belief in telling you the truth and empowering you at the same damn time. She is the CEO of BEC Production, an Event Production & Execution Agency, serving the Atlanta area and beyond. Ashley has been a decade long contributor to her beloved special events industry in a plethora of avenues. For years, she served as a member of International Live Events Association (ILEA), the Planning Committee of the Allies Awards, and is an annual speaker for Clayton State University Event Planning program. Ashley has been blessed to teach and encourage others in a variety of settings, from seminars, workshops, masterminds, and more.

She's also been awarded accolades from Atlanta Tribune Magazine, Modern Luxury Diamond Awards, and has been featured in a variety of publications like BlackBride.com, The Celebration Society, and Love Inc. Magazine to name a few.

Whether it's planning a fabulous wedding, multiple day conference, corporate client's brand activations, helping novice event professionals gain experience in the field, or helping fellow small business owners as a business consultant; Ashley is in her element.

Her passion is definitely challenging her clients and others to be their best selves in the present moment. Living life to the max, on your own terms, is Ashley Adana's philosophy.

Want to be a stockist? Book Ashley, or just get in touch:

AshleyAdana.com
hello@ashleyadana.com
Instagram: @Ashley_Adana

Index

A

Ashley Adana, Jan 7, Jan 19, Feb 15, Mar 12, Mar 23, Apr 19, Apr 21, Apr 24, May 14, Jun 11, Jun 21, Jul 4, Jul 11, Aug 5, Aug 17, Sept 23, Oct 22, Nov 24, Dec 22
Muhammad Ali, Jan 18, Dec 15
Debbie Allen, Jan 16, May 13
Maya Angelou, Mar 1, Apr 4, Jul 3, Jul 13, Aug 28, Oct 31
Arthur Ashe, Feb 7

B

Erykah Badu, Feb 26
Josephine Baker, Jun 4, Oct 11
James Baldwin, Feb 22, Aug 7
Tyra Banks, Mar 31
Angela Bassett, Sept 29
Harry Belafonte, Mar 2, Oct 26
André Benjamin, May 27
Roderick Benson, Sept 12
Halle Berry, Aug 13
Mary McLeod Bethune, July 10
Frankie Beverly, Dec 6
Yasiin Bey, Mar 30, Dec 11
Beyoncé, Feb 2, Aug 2, Dec 8
Simone Biles, Mar 17
Mary J. Blige, Jan 11, Jul 14
Sharon Bolden, Oct 12
Lisa Bonet, Nov 16
Cory Booker, Jun 9, Jul 12, Oct 21
Les Brown, Feb 16, May 8, Aug 29, Nov 3
Kobe Bryant, Feb 5, May 1, Aug 23, Nov 12, Dec 26
Ursula Burns, Sept 20

C

Diahann Carroll, July 17, Dec 12
Kenneth Chenault, Jul 24
Shirley Chisholm, Nov 30
Ciara, Oct 25
J. Cole, Mar 28, Jul 9
Marva Collins, Aug 31
Sean "Diddy" Combs, Jul 16, Nov 4
Common, Mar 13, Jul 27
Laverne Cox, May 29
Ice Cube, Jun 15, Mar 22

D

Stephanie Daniels, Jul 5
Angela Davis, Jan 26
Nehemiah Davis, Apr 16
Viola Davis, Aug 11, Nov 5
Ruby Dee, Oct 27, Feb 28
LaShonda Dixon, Sept 10
Dominique Dolyce, Sept 4
Frederick Douglass, Feb 25
Dr. Dre, Feb 13
Katherine Dunham, Jun 22
Victor Durrah, Jr., Apr 29
Ava Duvernay, Jun 18, Aug 24
Michael Eric Dyson, May 11, Oct 23

E

Marian Wright Edelman, June 6

Idris Elba, Sept 6, Apr 26
Duke Ellington, Apr 30
Missy Elliott, Jul 1
Jay Ellis, Dec 27
Wilfred Emmanuel-Jones, Nov 20

F
Ella Fitzgerald, Apr 25
Jamie Foxx, Mar 19, Dec 13
Jamie Fuller, Nov 1

G
Althea Gibson, Aug 27
Nikki Giovanni, Jun 7
Malcolm Gladwell, Sept 17
Shondra Glover, Nov 19
Whoopi Goldberg, Jun 10, Nov 13
Meagan Good, Aug 8
Berry Gordy, Nov 28
Earl G. Graves, Sr., May 31
CeeLo Green, May 30, Sept 9
Jasmine Guy, May 28, Oct 15

H
Regina Hall, Apr 11
Tamron Hall, Sept 16
Vincent Hall, Jul 15
Fannie Lou Hamer, Oct 6
Lorraine Hansberry, May 20
Janel Grant Hanserd, Jun 20
Hill Harper, Jun 28, Oct 14, Dec 18
Kamala Harris, Oct 20
T.I. Harris, Apr 13, Oct 3
Kevin Hart, Jan 24, Apr 23, Jul 6
Steve Harvey, Mar 3, May 12, Sept 22, Oct 18, Nov 18
Aaliyah Haughton, Sept 2

Taraji P. Henson, Sept 11, Nov 22
Lauryn Hill, May 26
Gregory Hines, Dec 31
Bell Hooks, Sept 24
Lena Horne, June 29
Whitney Houston, Aug 21
Janice Bryant Howroyd, Sept 1
Cathy Hughes, Apr 22
Langston Hughes, Mar 25
D. L. Hughley, Mar 6, Jun 14
Nipsey Hussle, Jan 27, Apr 10, Aug 15, Nov 11

J
Janet Jackson, May 16
Jesse Jackson, Oct 8
Samuel L. Jackson, Mar 11, Dec 21
LeBron James, Mar 7, Dec 30
Mae Jemison, Oct 17
Jidenna, Jan 4, May 2
Bozoma Saint John, Jul 21
Arianna Johnson, Dec 23
Gail Johnson, Jun 2
Magic Johnson, Feb 8, Aug 14, Nov 14
Robert L. Johnson, Apr 6
Nasir Jones, Jun 12, Oct 1
Quincy Jones, Mar 14
Michael Jordan, Feb 17
Michael B. Jordan, Feb 9, Jul 20

K
Coretta Scott King, Apr 27
Dr. Martin L. King, Jr., Jan 1, Apr 17, Aug 18, Oct 9
Eartha Kitt, Feb 3, Mar 27, Jul 28
Leigh Meriweather Knight, Apr

20, Jul 25
Solange Knowles, Jun 24
Boris Kodjoe, Mar 8

L

Patti LaBelle, May 24
Kendrick Lamar, Jun 17, Aug 10, Oct 16
Queen Latifah, Jan 10, Mar 18, Dec 24
Spike Lee, Mar 20
Ari Lennox, Mar 26
Jenifer Lewis, Jan 25, Dec 9
John Lewis, Feb 12, Jun 5
Lizzo, Apr 28
Dr. Edward Lockhart III, Aug 24
Lauren London, Dec 5
Audre Lorde, Feb 24 Jean Lovett, Nov 7
Ludacris, Oct 19

M

Dr. I.E. Mack, Dec 17
Malcolm X, May 19
Nelson Mandela, Jul 18, Jan 3
Meghan Markle, Duchess of Sussex, Aug 20
Aisha Miller, Jan 15
Anika Miller, May 5
Anthony Miller, Sept 5
Derrick Miller, Sr., May 4
Myderia Miller-Tripp, Feb 11, Jun 3, Nov 10, Dec 30
Janelle Monae, Dec 1
Toni Morrison, Feb 23, Mar 15
Eddie Murphy, Apr 3, Sept 8

O

Michelle Obama, Jan 17, Dec 10
President Barack Obama, Jan 21, Apr 15, Aug 4, Nov 21
Qualena Odom-Royes, Mar 4
Jesse Owens, Sept 19

P

Rosa Parks, Feb 4
Teddy Pendergrass, May 22
Tyler Perry, Jan 22, Mar 15, Apr 7, May 23, Jul 23, Nov 2
Donna Pitts, Feb 6
Sidney Poitier, Feb 20, May 7, Sept 7, Oct 24
Billy Porter, Sept 21
Colin Powell, Mar 29
Francis Pruitt, Apr 8

R

Issa Rae, Jan 12, Mar 21, Jul 26, Sept 30, Oct 13
Cyril Ramaphosa, Nov 17
Phylicia Rashad, Jun 19
Jahi Rawlings, Jan 5
Della Reese, Jul 7, Dec 7
Shonda Rhimes, Jan 13
Rihanna, Feb 27
Robin Roberts, Nov 23
Diana Ross, May 15
Tracee Ellis Ross, Jan 2, Aug 1, Oct 29

S

Deion Sanders, Aug 9
Jill Scott, April 2
Amanda Seales, Apr 18

Yara Shahidi, Feb 10
Tupac Shakur, Jun 16, Oct 2, Dec 16
Shannon Sharpe, Jan 8, June 26, Aug 30, Nov 15
Russell Simmons, Feb 29, Jun 13, Aug 19, Oct 4, Dec 3
Nina Simone, Feb 21
John Singleton, Jan 6
Andrea Smith, Apr 14
Dr. E. Dewey Smith, Jr., Jun 30
Jada Pinkett Smith, Jan 14, May 6, Jul 2, Aug 26, Sept 18
Jillian Smith, Dec 25
Will Smith, Jul 22, Sept 25, Dec 29
Alberta Sneid, Feb 14, May 9
Malidoma Patrice Somé, Sept 27
Sister Souljah, Jan 28, Apr 1, Jul 30
Octavia Spencer, Jul 19
Jazmine Sullivan, April 9
D'Etta Sumlin, Sept 14

T
Jason Taylor, May 3
Orie Lovett Thornton, Feb 1
Stacey Tripp, Sept 28
Harriet Tubman, Mar 10
Tina Turner, Nov 26
Aaron Turpeau, Ph.D, Feb 19
Cicely Tyson, Jan 9, Jul 8, Dec 19

U
Gabrielle Union, Jan 20, Sept 3, Oct 28

V
Iyanla Vanzant, Jan 23, Mar 5, May 18, Jun 27, Aug 3, Sept 13, Nov 6, Dec 14

W
Lena Waithe, May 17, Oct 7
Alice Walker, Mar 9, Aug 12, Nov 27
Madam C.J. Walker, Dec 20
Christopher "Biggie Smalls" Wallace, May 21
Booker T. Washington, Apr 12
Denzel Washington, May 10, Aug 6, Dec 28
Kerry Washington, Jan 31
Maxine Waters, Aug 16, Nov 9
Cornel West, Jun 1
Forest Whitaker, Jun 8, Nov 25
Kimm White, July 31
Frankie Williams, Sr., Oct 30
Monde Williams, May 25
Pharrell Williams, Apr 5
Serena Williams, Sept 26
Keisha Wilson, Sept 15
Russell Wilson, Nov 29
Oprah Winfrey, Jan 29, Mar 16, Jun 25, Aug 22, Dec 2
Alfre Woodard, Nov 8
Shantanese Wornum-Miller, Feb 18

Z
Jay Z, Apr 26, Dec 4

www.ingramcontent.com/pod-product-compliance
Lightning Source LLC
Chambersburg PA
CBHW061205070526
44583CB00025B/3120